AMATEUR DRAMATICS

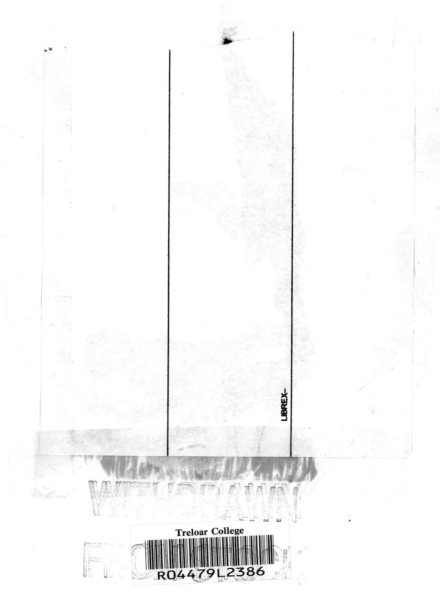

AMATEUR DRAMATICS

Jack Cassin-Scott

CASSELL

(*Cover photographs: Zoë Dominic/Catherine Ashmore*)

Also by Jack Cassin-Scott:

Costume and Fashion 1760–1920 (1971)
Models in the Making (1973)
Costume and Settings for Historical Plays
(Vols. 1–5) (1983)

A CASSELL BOOK

First published in the UK
1992 by Cassell
Villiers House
41/47 Strand
LONDON
WC2N 5JE

Reprinted 1993, 1994 (twice)
First paperback edition 1993

Distributed in the United States
by Sterling Publishing Co., Inc.
387 Park Avenue South, New York, NY 10016–8810

Distributed in Australia
by Capricorn Link (Australia) Pty Ltd
2/13 Carrington Road, Castle Hill, NSW 2154

British Library Cataloguing-in-Publication Data

Cassin-Scott, Jack
  Amateur Dramatics
  I. Title
  792.0226
  ISBN 0–304–34146–0
     0–304–34358–7 (*paperback*)

Typeset by Columns Design and Production Services Ltd,
Reading
Printed in Great Britain by The Bath Press, Avon

Contents

PREFACE   6

1 DESIGNING AND BUILDING
   THE SET   7
Introduction   7
The design process   8
The stage model   11
Stage positions   14
Flats   15
Painting the set   21

2 COSTUME   30
Introduction   30
Biblical and Egyptian   33
Greek and Roman   36
Post-Roman and Byzantine   40
Anglo-Saxon to Norman   45
Medieval   49
Renaissance   54
The sixteenth century   55
The seventeenth century   58
The eighteenth century   61
The nineteenth century   67
The early twentieth century   73
Headwear   77
Patterns and measurements   82

3 MAKE-UP AND WIGS   88
Introduction   88
Make-up   88
Wigs and hair   96
Period hairstyles and make-up   97

4 STAGE PROPS   104
Introduction   104
Materials and methods   104
Period stage furnishings   105
Modelling   110
Miscellaneous effects   122

5 LIGHTING AND SOUND
   EFFECTS   128
Introduction   128
Safety precautions   128
Period atmosphere   128
Lighting equipment   129
Designing the lighting   131
Special effects   132
Light intensity and colour   132
Miscellaneous lighting effects   134
Sound effects   136

GLOSSARY   137
BIBLIOGRAPHY   140
SUPPLIERS   141
INDEX   143

Preface

This is a book for the amateur theatre, written specifically for non-professional producers and designers of dramatic groups who wish to achieve the highest standards of stage technique but with the minimum of materials, stage dimensions, and finance and, perhaps, also without the help of skilled technicians. Although there is an irresistible magnetism to the 'back-stage' of theatre, some knowledge of theatrical working practice is needed for all those activities that go towards the complexity of a stage production, and a lack of this knowledge is one of the reasons many amateur productions fail.

The canvas back-cloth and the built wooden structures on the stage are commonly regarded as the 'scenery'. In reality, however, 'scenery' includes everything that makes the play come to life for the audience: costume, make-up, stage properties, lighting, etc. Also, in recent years, a great many innovations have been introduced into theatrical design, construction, and development, and the changes in scenic traditions that have occurred over the last two hundred years or so cannot be brushed aside if we are to understand these new ideas and skills: unless we have some knowledge of the past we can hardly expect to understand modern developments. We must also remember in any discussion about the stage that we are not referring to one particular thing or person but to several things and several people; in a nutshell, teamwork.

Always bear in mind as well that the art of theatre is the art of illusion: true realism is practically impossible. Many theatrical practitioners support the idea that what we should aim for is imaginative illusion suggested by abstract symbolic forms and colour, created by special effects to produce atmospheres. The spectators' imaginations should be stimulated by these symbolic forms, which should then lead them towards feeling the appropriate emotion. If we accept this we are not necessarily moving forward but, paradoxically, backwards in time: classical Greek theatre and much medieval theatre depended on such symbolism in costume and property to achieve their effects.

It is, however, difficult to weigh up the comparative merits of the different methods available to amateur stage productions: much will depend upon such factors as the time available, stage dimensions, artistic capabilities, and the skills of the team involved, as well as the financial outlay. The type of production will also dictate the treatment.

The following chapters, therefore, describe the available systems, giving an unbiased opinion about their advantages and disadvantages. The discussion includes the main areas of staging: the model, scenery design, building and painting, costume design and pattern-making, the art of make-up, stage properties, and, finally, lighting—the youngest of the theatre arts and considered today to be one of the most important.

1
Designing and building the set

INTRODUCTION

The design and creation of a play's staging begins with a play reading. From this the director and the production team start to put their ideas into practice, forming, through discussion, some rough ideas. Quick notes should be taken. Above all, total cohesion should be achieved between all concerned, whether director or designer—a single vision is an absolute necessity.

The performance space available to most amateurs is often very basic: a school hall with few or no technical amenities, perhaps simply a raised platform at one end of a hall. There could possibly be a stage with a framed arch front. However, the chief object at this time is the idea or concept—even with an unlimited budget and limitless space it is the quality of the ideas that is always the most important factor.

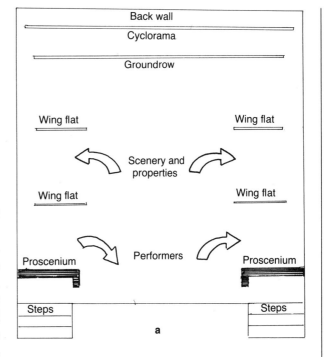

Figure 1.1 (a) It is important for everyone to remember where to exit and with what during scene changes to avoid delay and confusion; (b) proscenium-arch stage and sightlines

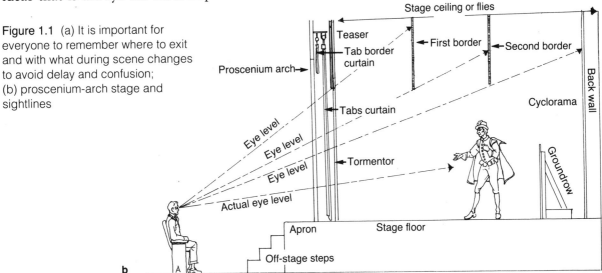

7

Before beginning a discussion of stage-scenery construction we must know something of the stage itself. While there are many types of stage, the usual concept that comes to mind is a box-shaped 'room' mounted on a platform that rises just over a metre or so from the ground (Figure 1.1). A structure with a rectangular opening similar to that of a picture frame covers the front of the stage area (the proscenium arch or opening). Immediately behind this is a curtain usually called the 'house curtain' or 'tabs'. This is often used to conceal scene changes. The spaces to the right and left of the proscenium are called the 'wings'. These (apart from the obvious entrances and exits) are used for lighting from the sides.

Sometimes, if height allows, there is a space above the stage (the 'flies') which contains a grid-iron. This grid-iron is a set of wooden beams that supports hanging scenery. Again if space permits, back-cloths can be hoisted up by means of ropes and pulleys. Under the stage can also be used for storing scenery and properties. The part of the stage that extends from the proscenium arch into the auditorium is called the apron. All stage measurements are derived from the proscenium opening.

The simplest setting is plain curtains or drapes, or a cyclorama sky-cloth and small cut-out stage-set pieces or groundrows. While being economic, this type of set can put a great strain on the players as the audience has no means of establishing the location of the action other than by oration from the performers. The play becomes more vocal than visual. This staging is reminiscent of Elizabethan playhouses and, while possibly being ideal for Shakespearian plays, it could fail for other productions. A 'standing set' (which remains in place throughout the whole play) presents no great difficulties other than with exit and entrance openings. In productions with two or more sets, the scenery and properties (props) must be designed so that they can be moved easily and quickly either to another part of the stage or removed completely. Irrespective of the available area, the scenery must be easily manoeuvrable for the stage staff and must conform to the players' proportions.

THE DESIGN PROCESS

Nothing is worse for an audience than waiting through seemingly unrehearsed set changes. These destroy the dramatic flow of the play. The set must, therefore, be flexible and simply designed to allow the audience to follow the action of the play without unnecessary delays. This is the prime requirement; it should be taken into account before anything else is considered.

The designer, unlike the actor, finds his or her expression not in words but in setting and costume: the set acts as a foundation from which all the other elements of the production emerge. After flexibility, the next consideration is the period of the play. Here comes the essential job of research. If this is done in a firm and diligent manner, the production will be much more professional. A careful study of period detail will result in a design worthy of the play.

Each production is a challenge, and each design is an individual creation. To begin with, study books on architecture; these are the designer's tools. A good designer must be an imaginative draughtsperson and technician and, although staging a play is a teamwork effort, the designer must be able to understand and hence guide the team's technical expertise. Designers must have, at their finger tips, an understanding of perspective, architecture, and (if the costumes are part of the designer's job) anatomy. The designer must be able to turn his or her hands to any of the applied arts—scenic design being only one. If the designer is not involved in the costumes, then he or she must remember that set design is as important as the costumes: both must reflect the trends and attitudes of the period.

The set design's function is to be a background to the play and it must therefore convey the correct atmosphere and mood of the play from the outset. Theatre (perhaps more than any other media) is larger than life: hence an irrelevant design, regardless of its artistic merit, will make no impact on the audience. A good stage set will appeal to the audience's imagination and transport them from ordinary, everyday life to the fantasy world of the play—the essence of a good design is its dramatic effect. As the design is a 'picture' of the proposed set, all its elements must be correctly balanced to achieve a practical, visual effect. The media to create this must, therefore, be carefully thought out. The five facets of theatre (performer, set, props, lighting, and make-up) must be used intelligently.

Deciding on the acting area is, obviously, one of the first items on the designer's and producer's agenda. For example, large halls and school gymnasiums are ideal for floor-level, 'theatre-in-the-round' productions, where the stage is surrounded on all four sides with three or four rows of seats, giving the audience a clear view of the 'stage'. This type of staging brings the audience closer to the action. This is ideal for pageant plays or plays where there is a large number of performers dancing or involved in choral routines. Scenery as such must, of necessity, be kept to the minimum; any movement of props and scenery becomes an added activity for the performers and must, for smooth presentation, be as well rehearsed as any role in the play.

The design, while emphasizing the atmosphere of the play, must (at the same time) remain subservient to the play itself—as must all the other facets of theatre. When interpreting the script, the designer must also be well acquainted with the director's ideas for the performers' movements. The script is simply the bare bones of the play: the set, the players' actions, and so on, are the flesh of the performance. Once all these are established, the designer can make a start on the ground plan.

Whatever the space available, this must be measured accurately and recorded on the first main plan to be drawn up—the ground plan. This can be drawn to a scale most convenient to the designer (1 in–1 ft or 2.5–30 cm is the ideal). Stage areas—whether amateur or professional—have a limited area for setting scenery and props.

The first, basic problem will be designing a ground plan that will allow the performers to move about comfortably. Here the designer is faced with the difficulty of keeping acting space free while, at the same time, attempting to create a convincing location. The more realistic the set, the greater this problem will be. A thorough knowledge of stage positions is essential, as a designer must know the effectiveness of certain stage positions that will allow the players the opportunity to enhance their performances effectively.

The designer should study the stage area closely, checking the sightlines from the audience to make sure there are no obstructions that will obscure any of the performers: audiences do not take kindly to an actor who is only a disembodied voice. As some areas of the stage are more important than others, the designer ensures that an important entrance or exit is not masked by a useless decorative piece of design. Whatever the shape of the stage area, the same principles apply.

The ground plan having been completed, the designer can now design the set or sets. Before starting, he or she must be quite sure of the play's action: consulting the director and a careful reading of the script should produce the final decision about the design. It is important to bear in mind the play's period, its time of day, exits, entrances, the position of props, and so on. Although this may seem rather obvious, behind these considerations lie the basic problems about the script's actual perception. Hidden details may only emerge from the dialogue when a performer actually refers to them or, conversely, details may not actually be referred to but are needed in order that dialogue may produce some action. The designer must visualize from the script all the things the performers refer to or use and, once again, the script is the focal point of reference. The playwright's stage directions often give a great deal of detail about the setting but these directions often contain unnecessary detail about atmosphere that reveals no action. The designer must, therefore, after consultation with the director, be free to reject anything that is considered to be superfluous.

All theatrical settings are three dimensional (Figure 1.2). To rely on a two-dimensional plan

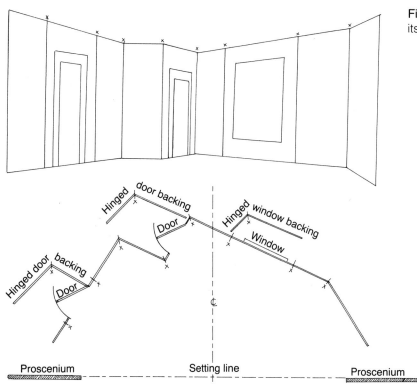

Figure 1.2 Proposed interior set and its ground plan

Hinged door backing

Door

Hinged window backing

Window

Hinged door backing

Door

₵

Proscenium

Setting line

Proscenium

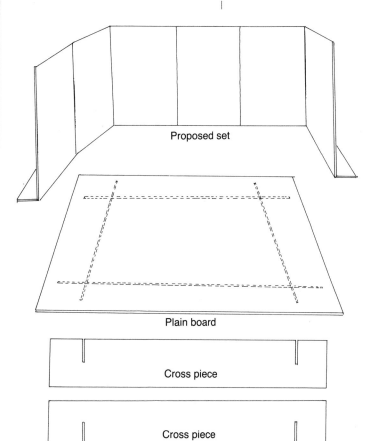

Figure 1.3 Basic stage platform

Proposed set

Plain board

Cross piece

Cross piece

will create untold problems. Confining work just to paper will be too restrictive: the finished design would remain too flat when construction is begun. It is advisable, therefore, to build a scale model of the set.

THE STAGE MODEL

The stage model should be a miniature scaled set on the stage it is to occupy. It is usually made from card or stiff board. It is painted and the props (furniture, etc.) are constructed and laid out in their positions to make the model as near as possible to the real thing. Using both the stage area's ground plan and the finished design drawing, the designer can now create such a model.

A model of a raised plain stage at the end of a hall is easily constructed. Cross pieces scaled to the height of the stage platform and a plain

board resting on top of this becomes the basic stage platform (see Figure 1.3). However, a fixed proscenium-arch stage (with or without an apron) allows for a more detailed model and more accurate measurements. A rostrum-built stage for a theatre-in-the-round at ground-floor level is shown in Figure 1.4. Whatever the stage area, the basic model-making tools are as follows:

- Sheets of white card.
- Ruler (metric and imperial).
- Metal straight edge.
- Set square.
- Compasses.
- 3H pencil.
- Scissors.
- Stanley-type modelling knife or designer's scalpel.
- Cutting board.
- Contact adhesive.

Figure 1.4 Large, flat, open area with a simple design that incorporates entrances and exits through the use of aisles. To overcome the viewing problem, rostra can be placed in the acting area to provide good sightlines

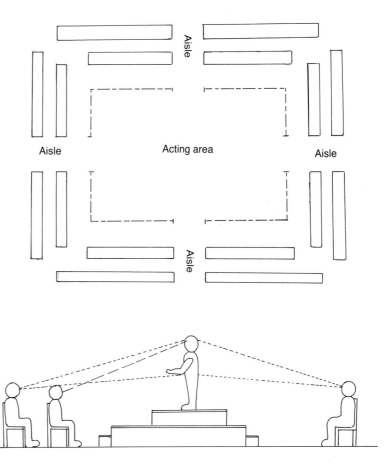

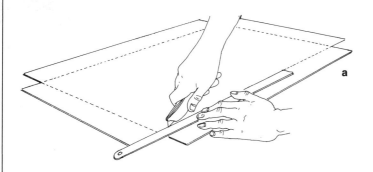

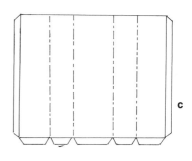

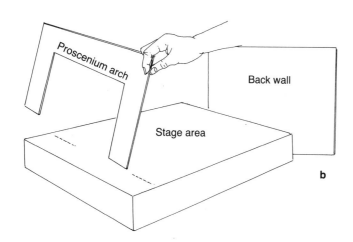

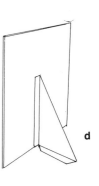

- Modelling clay (slow drying).
- Spray paints, gouache paints.
- Paint brushes (various).
- Thin balsa wood.
- Clear acrylic plastic.
- Masking tape.
- Erasers.
- Modelling tools.

It is useful at first to make a three-dimensional rough model with card, scissors, and masking tape to overcome some tantalizing problem that seems unfathomable and when thinking on the matter is undecided. A good, rough model can suggest a solution before the proper model is made and, of course, can also create them!

The final model can now be carefully cut out from the drawn, scale pieces (Figure 1.5). The metal straight edge and a very sharp blade should be used to cut the card accurately (Figure 1.6). A self-healing cutting board is ideal for protecting blades and table tops. (A word of warning to those unused to scoring or cutting with knives: keep fingers behind the blade!) The card is bent by cutting through the board and then bending it away from the cutting line. Steps or stairs are made by cutting each tread or riser alternately, and this will then bend itself into the desired form. With quick-drying contact adhesives, the cut-out pieces can be assembled quickly (Figure 1.6).

Details of moulding, and so on, can be added

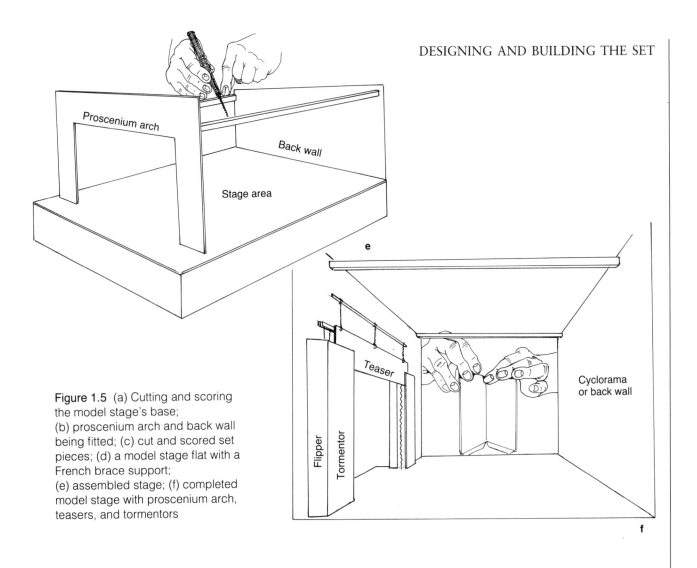

Figure 1.5 (a) Cutting and scoring the model stage's base; (b) proscenium arch and back wall being fitted; (c) cut and scored set pieces; (d) a model stage flat with a French brace support; (e) assembled stage; (f) completed model stage with proscenium arch, teasers, and tormentors

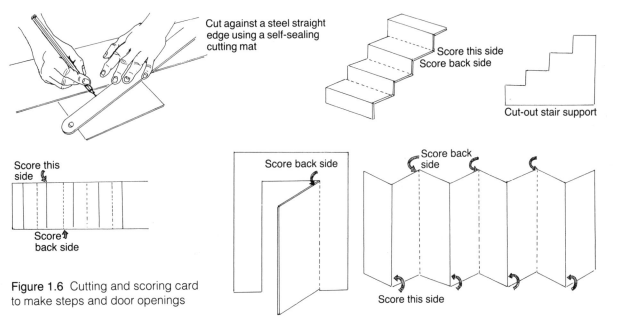

Figure 1.6 Cutting and scoring card to make steps and door openings

with strips of balsa wood in varying thicknesses. Banisters and balustrades can be made from drinking-straws or whatever materials are readily available. Curtains and drapes can be made from tissue paper dipped in glue or paste and then contoured to give it a convincing appearance. (Figure 1.7 shows such period details.)

Exteriors covered with foliage can be made very convincingly by using model-makers' sphagnum moss coloured to the desired shade; plastic plants can be used to blend in to the scene. In the past it was always difficult for amateurs to produce either a fog-bound marshland or a dream sequence, but now dry-ice machines are available commercially as compact units that can be hired from most theatrical electrical suppliers (more information about these and other special effects will be found in Chapter 4). A small smoke tablet will suffice to create the desired effect in the finished model.

Model props (tables, chairs, bookcases, etc.) can be made to scale from board and fitted into the interior of the model. Slow-drying modelling clay, when baked, can be made into cushions (for example, *chaise longue* sausage-shaped cushions). Again, many small household items, such as screws, small bolts, washers, beads, etc., can be pressed into service.

It is the designer's job to communicate with the director and performers by showing them the exact layout of the set down to the last, minute detail. If the model is sufficiently well made, it will help in any dialogue. The set-builders' needs can also be explained and the performers will be able to visualize their acting positions. The model will also show whether or not the exits and entrances are in satisfactory places and if there is sufficient space for the stage crew to make all the necessary changes. Most importantly, all sightlines should be unhindered by any obstruction and, from the audience's point of view, all acting areas should be visible (this will save countless hours of rehearsal). In summary, the model must meet all the practical requirements of the play: it should show these with the greatest effect but with the least effort and expenditure.

STAGE POSITIONS

The floor area of the stage (which is usually a rectangle) has a language of its own, and this should be understood thoroughly before the set is designed. Such terms as upstage, downstage, stage right, etc., may seem confusing because, to the designer sitting in the audience, they are opposite to the designer's own left and right. Stage directions are, traditionally, always given from the actor's point of view (see Figure 1.8).

Figure 1.7 Period details:
(a) Victorian latch window with half-drawn curtain; (b) large windows, double-draped curtains; (c) baluster, 1860–5; (d) Victorian iron baluster

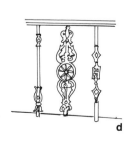

Figure 1.8 Stage positions: on stage—entrance to stage; centre line—centre line of stage; off stage—exit from stage; skycloth—backdrop or cyclorama. Positions on stage: (A) up right (UR); (B) up centre right (UCR); (C) up centre (UC); (D) up centre left (UCL); (E) up left (UL); (F) centre right (CR); (G) centre stage (CS); (H) centre left (CL). Onstage (either side) towards centre stage; offstage (either side) from centre stage. (I) Down right (DR); (J) down centre right (DCR); (K) down centre (DC); (L) down centre left (DCL); (M) down left (DL). OP—opposite prompt corner; PS—Prompt corner (traditional working side). Apron—space in front of the proscenium arch

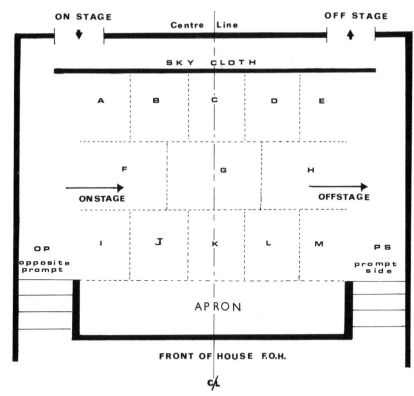

To confuse things further, the terms 'offstage' and 'off stage' can have different meanings. When an object or performer moves away from the centre of the stage, this is moving 'offstage', but when the object or performer leaves the stage completely, this is 'off stage'.

If the stage has a proscenium arch and an apron, then stage jargon becomes even more confusing. Terms such as 'teaser' and 'tormentor' can be perplexing (especially so as no one seems to know their origins), but they are an important part of most permanent stage fixtures. 'Teasers' mask the flies or upper structures, while 'tormentors' mask the wing areas. A 'flipper' is a narrow piece of scenery that supports a tormentor in an upright position.

FLATS

The traditional constituent parts of stage sets are flats—simple rectangular frameworks of wood covered in canvas upon which scenes are painted, and which replace the draperies formerly used to mask backstage activities (Figure 1.9(a)). Deciding on the size of the flats to be made is really a matter of the stage area to be covered and the available height. The basic flat unit, for practical purposes, should be as lightweight and as manageable as possible. An ideal size is between 7 and 9 ft (2 and 2.7 m) in height and 3 to 4 ft (1–1.2 m) in width. These units can be cleated together or hinged (Figure 1.9(b)), although hinging makes flats much heavier as they are now doubled in size. Hinging is, however, ideal for 'quick' booking pieces (see later), especially for door backings or corner pieces.

The flat's frame is usually made of white pine wood, 3 × 1 in (7.5 × 2.5 cm), cut to the required lengths. Two stiles are cut for the uprights and two rails to go across the top and bottom. To strengthen this frame, a toggle rail is inserted in the centre. Obviously, the taller the flat, the more toggle rails must be inserted. For amateur productions, the height does not usually exceed 9 ft (2.7 m) and so only a single toggle rail is needed.

Joints should be mortise and tenon for flats over 9 ft (2.7 m) high (Figure 1.9(c)). The

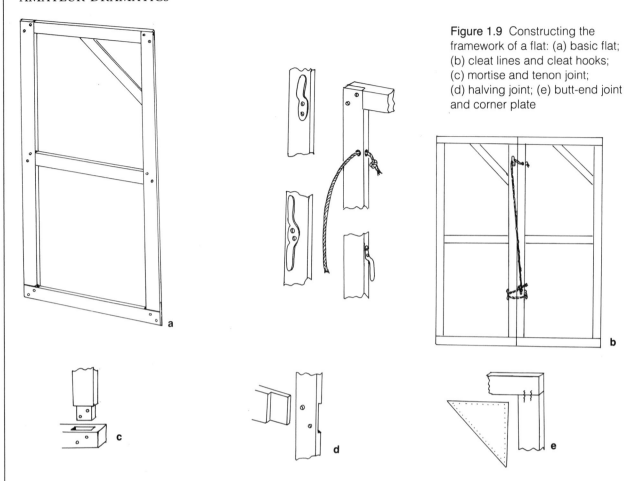

Figure 1.9 Constructing the framework of a flat: (a) basic flat; (b) cleat lines and cleat hooks; (c) mortise and tenon joint; (d) halving joint; (e) butt-end joint and corner plate

mortise is cut into the rail and the tenon into the stile. Toggle rails are cut in reverse order: the mortise is cut into the stile and the tenon into the rail (or just a halving joint is used—see Figure 1.9(d)). If necessary for greater rigidity, an angled cross piece can be inserted from one corner of the toggle rail to the stile (perhaps using simpler halved joints). All these joints must be glued and screwed. Another strengthening method is to use butt-end joints, which allows the stile and rail to be joined by 'wriggly' nails (Figure 1.9(e)). The joint is then covered by a flat triangular piece of plywood, which stengthens the joint by being nailed at each corner (Figure 1.9(e)).

Scenic canvas can be purchased in bales either 36 or 72 in (1 or 2 m) wide. After being measured carefully, this is cut to size and tacked to either the top or bottom rail. The canvas must be cut to the same size as the frame with no overlap whatsoever: it is better to be slightly under by about a quarter of an inch (half a centimetre) or so all round to prevent the canvas fraying when handled. The canvas is tacked to the inner edge of the rail batten leaving a 2½ in (6.5 cm) loose border. All four sides are now stretched and tacked down in the same way (Figure 1.10(a)). At each corner a 1½ in (4 cm) V-shape is cut out of the loose canvas to allow the corners to join evenly when the border is glued down to make a smooth join (Figure 1.10(b) and (c)). To smooth the canvas down, a rag dipped in hot water is run over the glued border (Figure 1.10(d)). When the glue has dried the canvas should be fairly taut.

As already mentioned, flats are joined together by cleats to create the required pieces of scenery (Figure 1.11(a)–(c)). Cleats are situated on the back of the stile about 18 in (45 cm) from the top. A hole is drilled obliquely into the stile on the left-hand side. Through this a sash-line or

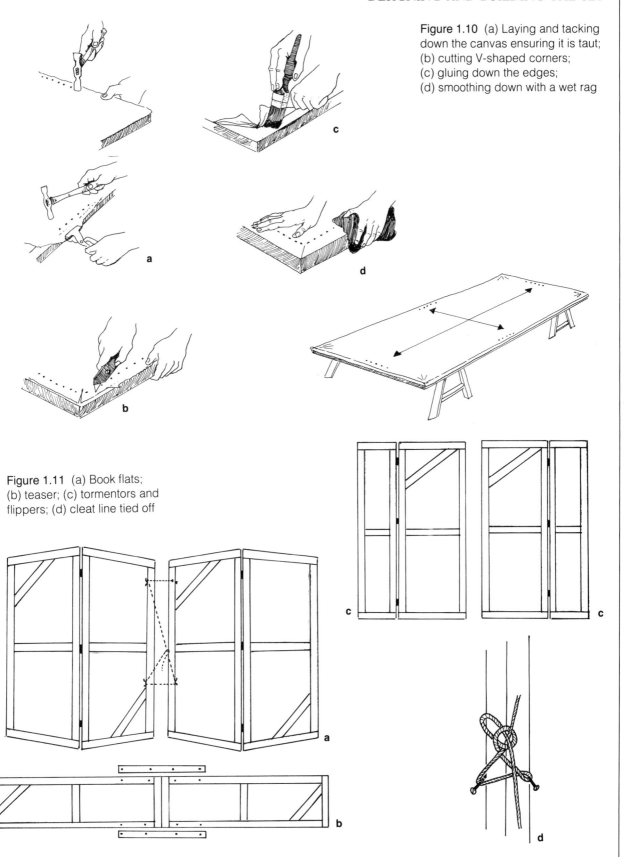

Figure 1.10 (a) Laying and tacking down the canvas ensuring it is taut; (b) cutting V-shaped corners; (c) gluing down the edges; (d) smoothing down with a wet rag

Figure 1.11 (a) Book flats; (b) teaser; (c) tormentors and flippers; (d) cleat line tied off

thin rope is inserted, which is pulled tightly and knotted securely on the inside and left to hang down. This is the cleat line. On the back right-hand side of the flat (at the same distance from the top) a metal hook is screwed in—the cleat hook. (These can also be made of wood.) Inside this stile, about 3 ft (1 m) from the bottom rail, a straight screw is inserted but left about 1 in (2.5 cm) or so proud of the stile. The means of joining flats together is now complete (Figure 1.9(b)). The cleat line is thrown over the cleat hook and pulled sharply and firmly down. This

is then hooked round the screws and cast through its own length. It is then pulled as taut as possible and tied off in an easily released slip knot (Figure 1.11(d)).

I mentioned earlier the hinged book flat, which consists of two flats hinged together by three 3 in (7.5 cm) hinges. The hinges are fixed onto the face side allowing the flats to be booked when the uncanvassed sides are on the outside. To hide the opening and hinges, it is advisable to cut a strip of canvas about 4 in (10 cm) wide and the length of the flat. Follow

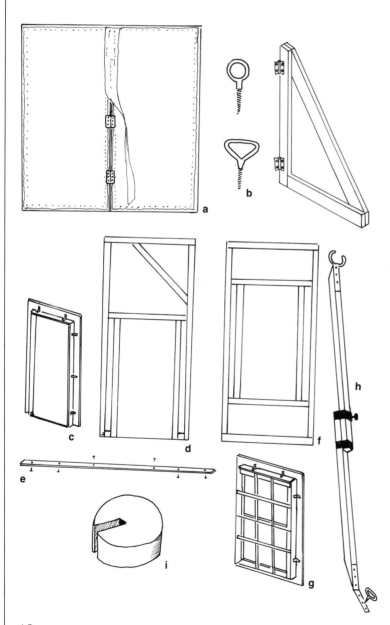

Figure 1.12 (a) Concealing hinges on a book flat; (b) stage screws and French brace, which is usually hinged to the flat to support it and weighted down with a stage weight (i); (c) door frame; (d) door flat; (e) iron door-sill; (f) window flat; (g) window piece; (h) brace; (i) stage weight

the same procedure for fixing canvas on the frame, tacking the canvas on the outer edge of each flat and down the centre joining. Now glue the narrow loose canvas strip firmly down (Figure 1.12(a)).

Flax (scenic canvas) is available in various widths. This is lightweight, tightly woven, and is ideal for backdrops and cycloramas as it has very little shrinkage. Hessian/burlap can also be used. This is cheaper but has many draw-backs: it is loosely woven, it shrinks, and it does not wear well. For ghost scenes, use scrim/gauze that has a wide mesh. Muslin is ideal for diffusing light.

White-pine timber (3×1 in or 7.5×2.5 cm) is the most practical and easy to handle. Plywood is expensive but reliable. Blockboard can be used as an alternative, but this is rather heavy. Hardboard is also too heavy for flats. All materials, however, must be fire-proofed. Interior scenes (box sets) can be made with various-sized flats, and their construction and support methods are shown in Figure 1.12(b)–(i). A selection of plain flats, door flats with

Figure 1.13 (a) Folding rostrum, here made to fold away with hinges; (b)–(d) constructing a ramp (which must be made strongly with mortise and tenon joints); (e) strong steps; (f) rostra steps; (g) 'cheese-piece' rostra

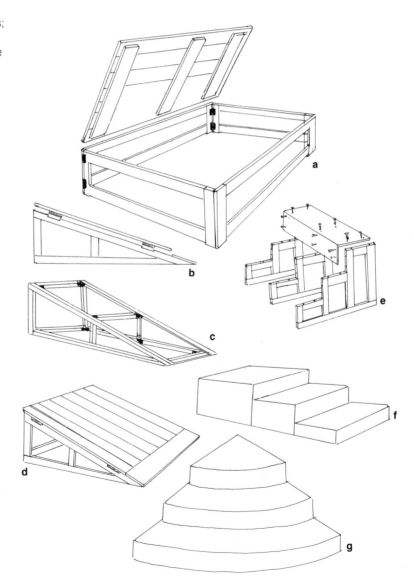

Figure 1.14 A simple Roman interior made from cut-out flats. This type of set, known as a cameo set-piece, is also suitable for small stages

Figure 1.15 A versatile set consisting of six flats and two 1 m rostra as steps. Additional hanging pieces convert this into a Roman Imperial palace

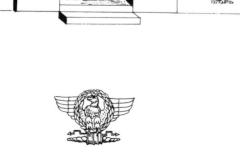

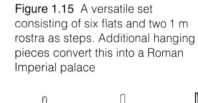

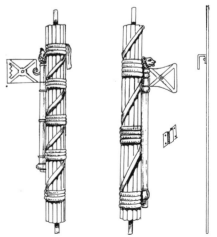

Figure 1.16 These types of architectural cut-out piece can represent cathedrals and castles: (a) simple arch on two-tier rostra steps; (b) arch on three rostra steps (ideal for a throne); (c) cathedral arch on rostra steps

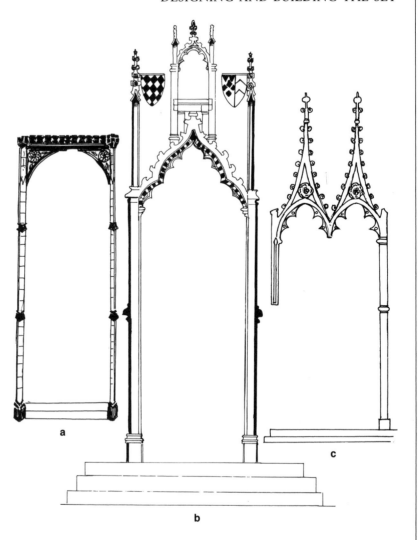

iron sills at the bottom, and filler flats for windows and openings (such as cupboards) is also shown. Figures 1.13–19 show the construction of other types of scenery.

Having built the flats, the canvas is now primed with a mixture of strong size and whitening. When dry the canvas will be extremely taut over the frame. The flats are now ready for painting.

PAINTING THE SET

Painting scenery is an art that improves with practice once the artist's inhibitions have been overcome. The set's area can be daunting, and scaling up from the original design to the actual set is perhaps at first difficult to contend with. With gains in confidence and the seeming freedom of movement, the wide brush strokes that are so much a part of stage painting soon turn the reluctant painter into an enthusiastic artist.

Various sizes of brushes are needed (Figure 1.20): a large 6-in (15-cm) brush for laying in the undercoat; a 4 × 3 in (10 cm × 7.5 cm) one for painting large areas; and a 2 × 1 in (5 × 2.5 cm) one for larger, detailed work. Finally, fitches of about 1.25 cm are very useful for finer detail and lining work. Buckets of different sizes are needed to hold paint for larger areas and for mixed glue size. Tins are useful to hold smaller quantities of paint, and odds and ends of sticks for stirring. Charcoal and coloured

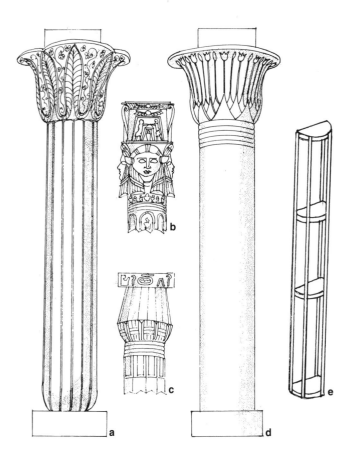

Figure 1.17 *Above* These movable heraldic cut-outs and crown pieces are ideal for historical and Shakespearian plays. Simple in construction, they can be slotted into rostra or placed behind throne stage pieces. Placed at varying heights on stage and individually lighted, they convey good theatrical atmosphere

Figure 1.18 Columns and capitals: (a) Egyptian bell capital with palm design, either painted or sculptured; (b) Egyptian Hathor bud capital (the head of a goddess supporting the model of a temple front); (c) Egyptian bud capital; (d) Egyptian bell capital in the form of lotus flowers, the emblem of the Upper Nile. The capital could also be in the form of papyrus, the emblem of the Lower Nile; (e) structure of a half-rounded pillar shape

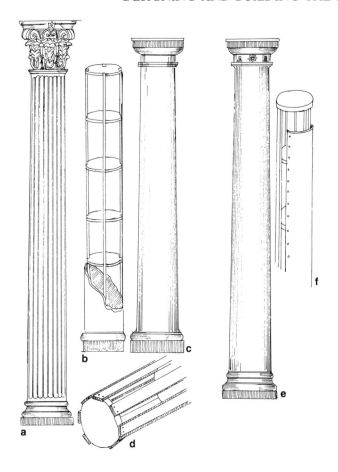

Figure 1.19 Columns and capitals:
(a) Greek Corinthian pillar; (b)
structure of pillar; (c) Roman Tuscan
pillar; (d) making a pillar in the
round; (e) Greek Doric column;
(f) covering the wooden pillar
structure with plywood or papier
mâché

chalk are needed for marking out on coloured backgrounds (charcoal is easier to 'flog off' with a duster, but try not to rub either off with your hand). A metre stick and a tape-measure are an essential part of the equipment. A double bevel-edged piece of wood about 3 ft (1 m) long and 3 in (7.5 cm) wide with a handle in its centre can be used as a straight edge. A plumb-line and mahl stick are also useful accessories. Because brushes are so expensive, they must be cared for and washed out thoroughly after each day's work (Figure 1.21).

As mentioned earlier, the canvas on the flats and the back-cloth or cyclorama needs a priming coat of white paint (glue size mixed with a whitening mixture). This coat gives a vibrancy to the final colours. To prepare this primer, first place the whitening in a bucket and cover it with water, allowing it to soak overnight. Next make up the glue size in a bucket (one part size to one part water), allow

it to soak, and then add about six parts boiling water to the soaked size and stir it thoroughly until the mixture has dissolved completely. Slowly add the size to the soaked whitening until a thick, cream consistency is achieved. As almost every part of the set is usually painted, this primer should be applied to everything that constitutes the set.

The drawings and models must now be placed in a safe position so that they are to hand as constant sources of reference and guidance. There are two methods of painting scenery: the upright method with the aid of step-ladders or scaffolding and the flat method where the back-cloth or flat is laid on the floor and painted with long-handled brushes. Both methods can be used successfully (Figure 1.22).

Scaling up is the same for both methods. To enlarge the designer's sketch of a back-cloth to the size required for the stage, square up the drawing to the measurement chosen. Transpose

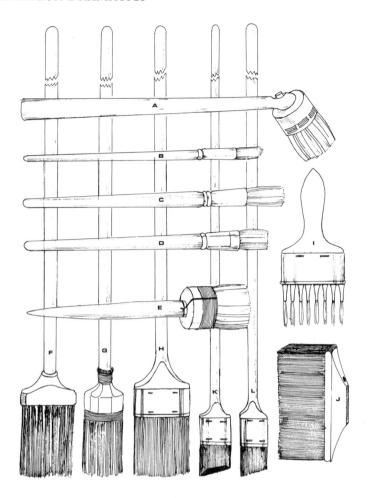

Figure 1.20 Brushes for scenery painting: (a) angle brush with handle; (b) four-sided liner; (c) long liner; (d) flat liner; (e) round scenery ring liner; (f) French-style scenic brush; (g) round sheath liner; (h) straight landscaper; (i) finger brush used for graining effect; (j) a theatre primer that can be fitted with handles; (k) a chiselled diagonal liner; (l) diagonal inking striker for lining work (most of these are made for both floor and upright painting. For floor work they are fitted with handles approximately 1 m long)

Figure 1.21 (a) A double bevel-edged scenic straight edge; (b) using the mahl stick; (c) a method of keeping brushes clean

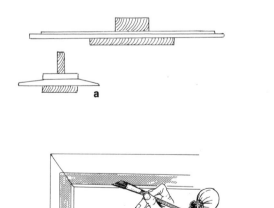

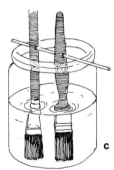

Figure 1.22 Painting in the upright position with step-ladders and a board and working on the floor with long-handled brushes

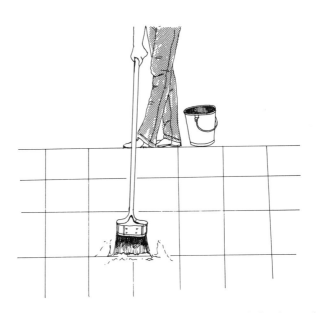

this squaring-up process to the back-cloth, and apply the same method to the flats. The squares guide the set painter because the large squares on the cloth represent what appears in the small squares on the design. Hence a faithful reproduction is achieved (Figure 1.23). A snap-line (a length of strong string covered with charcoal or chalk) is the simplest way of transposing the enlarged scale. Held taut on the measurement marks, the snap-line is plucked up in the centre and then allowed to snap back sharply, leaving a line impression on the cloth or flat's surface (Figure 1.24). For sketching in detail, it is easier to insert a stick of charcoal into a metal ferrule that is firmly secured to a long stick or, alternatively, into the open end of a long bamboo rod that is then tightly bound with string to hold the charcoal firmly in place. Both methods give good arm reach and freedom of movement (Figure 1.23).

There are other methods of applying paint apart from painting with brushes. Spraying can be used for large areas and is also useful in stencil work for wallpaper effects, etc. The spatter method is achieved by spattering paint from a fully charged brush. This is held in one hand and, while the palm of the other strikes the ferrule, this allows the paint to be flung from the brush. This is very effective for sky effects on a flat-painted body tone. The sponge method is quick and easy and gives a textured effect that softens the underlying colour. This

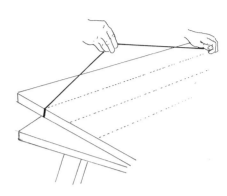

Figure 1.23 *Left* Squaring up the painting

Figure 1.24 *Above* Using a snap-line

method is applied by cutting an ordinary 10-in (25-cm) household sponge in half, leaving one side flat. This is dipped into the paint, wrung out, and then patted onto the surface of the painted cloth or flat. Different texture effects can be obtained by reversing the sponge onto its irregular side. Another method of texturing uses towelling material saturated with paint. This is rolled and twisted into a long, oblong shape and then applied to the painted surface by rolling it up and down. There are many other methods of producing textured surfaces, for example, using wood-chippings and sawdust. Although these are very effective they are not recommended for amateurs who may wish to re-use scenery for future productions. These methods are shown in Figure 1.25 for those interested.

The paint rollers now used by most house decorators can be employed effectively by the scenery painter. Rollers are labour saving when it comes to covering large areas, and they are also ideal for texturing. Sheepskin-covered rollers are very effective for large areas while cheaper varieties can be converted to achieve different effects. Figure 1.26 shows a few uses of the roller.

The paint used for scenery painting is usually tempera, which is made up from coloured chalk-like pigments derived from vegetable or mineral substances. This powder is mixed with glue size, which acts as a binding agent and is mixed in in the same way as primer. Tempera is used extensively in stage paintwork. It has a rapid drying time and dries to a dead-matt finish. Its only disadvantage, if it can be called such, is that the colour dries to a lighter tone than it was when wet (as do most commercial emulsion paints). A quick drying-test is always advisable, as the final tone could alter the whole concept of the set.

Aniline dyes are used extensively in the theatre for all kinds of materials—for curtains and back-cloths that can subsequently be folded and stored and also for drapes and costumes. These dyes (which have a chemical pigment and a binding agent) are dissolved in water before being applied thinly to the material's surface. The colours they produce are brilliant and they leave the material soft and pliable. Their great disadvantage is that, in time, they fade under the strong light of theatre lamps and they are also very difficult to paint over for any future productions.

Scenery painting is the reverse of water-colour painting: in scenery painting the dark colours are laid in first (these being used mainly in the foreground to give a hard definition), and then bright highlights are applied to bring out the dimensional effect. Shadowing is important in painting 'room' sets (panelling, doors, and door frames, etc.) but, before painting this,

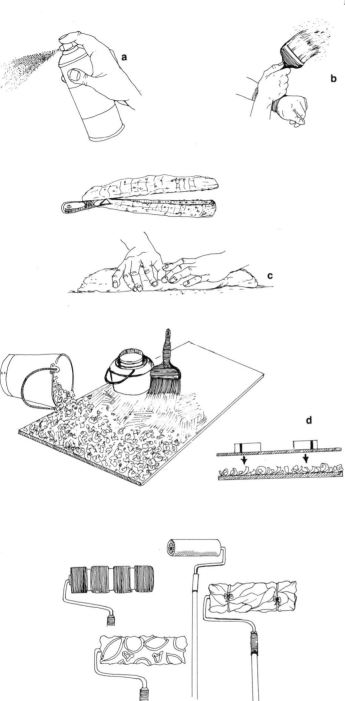

Figure 1.25 (a) The spray method; (b) the brush-splatter method; (c) the sponge method; (d) reproducing a textured surface with size and wood chippings that are then weighted down with a board and stage weights; (e) a dry brushing technique; (f) a brush being used for stippling

Figure 1.26 *Left* Paint rollers used for scenic work, either normally or cut to various patterns

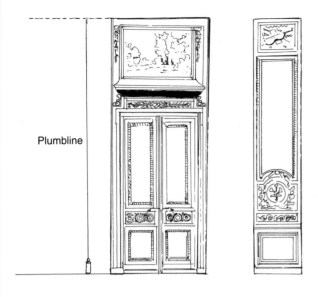

Plumbline

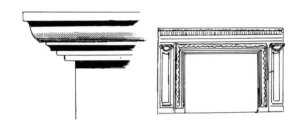

make sure all lines are straight—whether parallel or vertical—as slanting or crooked lines show out dreadfully when viewed from the audience (here the snap-line and plumb-line play their part). It is always advisable to measure from stage-floor level upwards: study a piece of moulding and observe the depth of shadow lines (Figure 1.27 shows some examples). Figure 1.28 shows the alternative of using real, ready-made mouldings.

Countrysides change from period to period, and so details of fields, hedgerows, and background architecture must be researched carefully (although audiences come to enjoy the efforts of an amateur production they are also the most vehement of critics!). The sky is always a problem and, very often, a source of discouragement to the scenery painter. A dramatic, beautifully painted floating mass of clouds is entirely unnecessary—real skies are changing constantly. Painting a plain, even tone overall is much better as it allows the lighting people the opportunity to produce a variety of lighting effects. It is worth while to have a taut cyclorama running along the back of the stage,

Figure 1.27 *Above* Painted shadows and panel decoration, about 1800

Figure 1.28 Examples of ready-made mouldings and window pieces in fibre glass or latex: (a) Tudor arch; (b) bead-and-reel moulding; (c) diamond-paned leaded light; (d) Gothic stone window; (e) Tudor leaded light

curved about the sides and top (Figure 1.29). The material for this is usually bound and eyeletted, and held taut on a tubular metal frame by being laced with strong elastic bands. Groundrows can then be used in front of this (Figure 1.30).

Cloud machines are available—a projector lamp that has a disc in front of it that slowly rotates by a small motor. The cloud and sky effects on the disc (aided by the curved cyclorama) give a convincing impression of endlessly moving clouds. Realistic effects of rolling waves on a sea can also be produced in this way. The designer can make good use of this type of machine to create beautiful atmospheric effects that become a vibrant part of the overall design (more about these special effects is discussed in Chapter 5).

Figure 1.29 A cyclorama stretched taut on a tubular frame

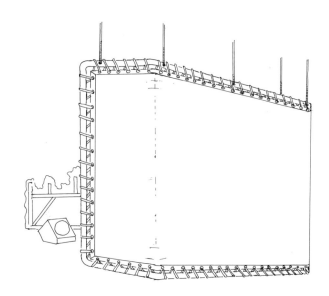

Figure 1.30 Profile groundrows for use in front of a cyclorama

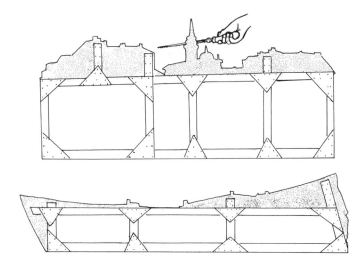

2
Costume

INTRODUCTION

Designing stage costumes begins immediately after the play reading and before the first production meeting. At this stage a rough sketch of the basic costumes is sufficient, and this will help in forming an early idea of how the characters will be dressed. In designing the costumes it is important to remember that clothes are worn not merely because they are necessary but also because they represent the character's social status, and above all, the individual's character. The main function of theatrical costumes is to help the performer portray the character they are acting. Costume designers should acquire an encyclopaedic knowledge of the period's costumes and apply strong imagination to their design.

Before a performer's voice is heard, the audience learns a great deal from the character's appearance. In dance this is even more important, where usually a lack of speech means a dancer's costume must convey the correct impression. Here the visual effect of style and colour, if the costume is designed correctly, will become an extension of the dancer's movements.

In a play the script will usually give an idea of the number of costumes required. Take note of the playwrights' directions, which may refer to costume, lapses of time, a reversal of social position, or some underlying aspect of a character that needs bringing out-for example, a comic character may need an exaggerated costume. Wigs and shoes also require careful research.

While the main purpose of this section is a guide to designing and making suitable costumes simply and practically, an understanding of social history is important if the costumes are to be accurate. It is not meticulous detail but the overall effect that is most important. In simple terms, a theatrical costume is the arrangement of materials in a particular way to express the style of a period. It is the costume designer's task to reinforce the dramatic tension of the play.

Costumes make a powerful impact and must never be underestimated: a badly designed garment can hinder the performer in expressing the character. The temptation to be over-elaborate should be resisted—all that is really necessary is contrast created by bold colours and shapes that suggest clothes that are really worn. If this is achieved there is no need to spend time chasing greatly detailed authenticity. Costumes should be reduced to their essentials, and most designers will find more than enough in galleries and libraries to occupy the time they have available for research.

Exaggerating line and colour must be part of the designer's brief for, without this, the impact of a character and his or her costume would be lost in the background. The thing to remember is that costuming is like the scenery—larger than life and used to convey characterization. The costume's design tells the audience all there is to know about the character's role, occupation, and social standing, etc.

The important factors in designing and making theatrical costumes are time, finance, and the available materials. Materials should be chosen for their texture and suitability of colour. Texture is particularly important on the stage, especially in relation to how it reads from a distance and under stage lighting. Materials that possess these qualities are not always easy to find, but the sensible use of furnishing fabrics, linen, blanket material, and hessian (to mention just a few) would perhaps result in the correct effects on stage.

A suitable workshop or wardrobe room should first be made available that is fitted out to produce the costumes and maintain them through the scheduled number of performances. The basic facilities should include some form of water supply (a sink or wash basin with hot and cold water), good illumination and ventilation, and a safe electrical source. Essential equipment includes a sewing machine, ironing board and iron, drying rack, costume rails, and as many coat hangers as possible (a spin-dryer would also be an asset). Plastic bowls and buckets, dyes, paints, sprays of various colours, and brushes are also needed, and no wardrobe department would be complete without the obvious needles, cotton, elastic, scissors, measuring tape, and pins. Latex adhesive and oddments of braids and other materials will also be useful, and most important are a large table or working surface and a full-length mirror.

If the production's emphasis is on realism, then historical accuracy will not be enough—dramatic reality must be achieved to create theatrical effectiveness. If the style is abstract, on the other hand, the emphasis must be on the texture and colour: trimmings and ornamentation must be kept to the minimum and the costumes kept simple and symbolic. Flowing silks, muslin, and soft fabrics are part of the psychological power of the abstract, along with unusual and imaginative outline forms. However, nothing should replace or overwhelm the performer or the role. In a realistic production, an imitation of nature should be adopted. Personalities can be exaggerated but they must remain recognizable characters from real life—not over-dressed, animated puppets. Costume details should be heightened to achieve

the correct sense of period. Historical periods may, however, be interwoven, but there must always be a clear, basic, sense of reality.

Before making the costumes, look first in second-hand shops as they could have just the right costume that needs little or no alteration. Charity shops, street markets, and jumble sales are good sources of cheap oddments. Clothes obtained here are, of course, useful mainly for late Victorian or modern productions but, with a little imagination, some could be adapted as period costumes.

If the costuming decided upon are the type of clothes worn in the present day, it is perhaps simpler to borrow or hire them. However, if the designer feels that certain qualities in the character's costume need emphasizing, then it may be worth while to create something original. If the production is set in a historical period then most costumes must be hired or made. Hiring, however, can be very expensive. If the production team wants to continue to produce plays then making costumes can be contemplated in the knowledge that future productions will be able to benefit from alterations and adjustments to already-made costumes.

Once the style has been decided and the parts cast, realizing the costumes begins. The wardrobe department should be given the completed costume sketches and notes on fabrics and decoration, which should be clearly explained, and the approximate lengths of materials and trimmings. It is always better to buy a cheaper, thinner fabric and to line this with remnants than to purchase an expensive one and lose the fullness and flow of the costume. The choice of fabric will depend on the correct texture for the wearer's personality and social position. Many different textures will be needed to create the right effect and the best surface qualities. Materials should be substantial enough not to need backing. A variety of weaves will lend interest to the design. Contrasting coarse surfaces with fine ones and matt surfaces with shiny ones will enliven costumes. Surface qualities can be altered by the use of paint and glue and by fringing, quilting, overlays, and appliqués.

It is sometimes difficult to find the right

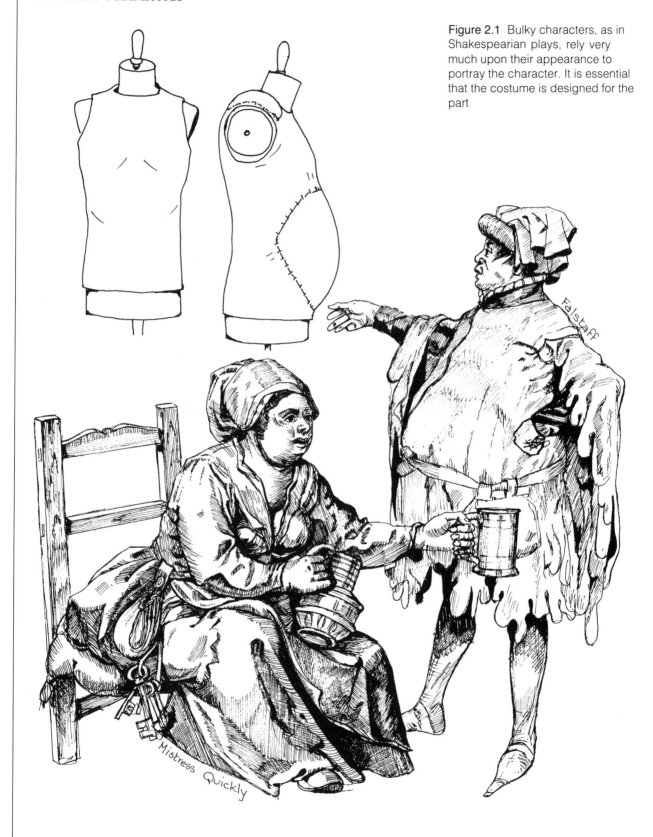

Figure 2.1 Bulky characters, as in Shakespearian plays, rely very much upon their appearance to portray the character. It is essential that the costume is designed for the part

fabric for a particular costume. Changing and disguise must therefore be employed. Dyeing, stencilling, or appliqué can all be used. Household dyes can give excellent results. A stencil cut out of strong paper will enable a pattern to be repeated over the fabric. Fabric paint can be applied with either a brush or a spray. Appliqué is another useful means of changing materials, but it is very time consuming. The appliqué can be stuck with adhesive to save time but this makes the garment virtually uncleanable.

To make good patterns, first cut out a length of material and make a miniature garment by draping and pinning it on a small lay figure, which can be purchased at any art shop. Trace the results on squared paper. It is best to make the patterns first out of brown paper or newspaper and then enlarge these to the measurements of the actual wearer.

Constructing a stage costume is different from dress-making. Dress-making involves adapting a garment to a particular person; in making a stage costume, however, the character is fitted to the garment. In fashion design the latest trends are of the upmost importance; stage costumes are only concerned with the character and the atmosphere of, usually, a bygone era. Consider the character first and then create the costume with the role the character must play foremost in your mind. Stage costumes are an integral part of the stage picture and they are characterized by their structure—in essence, their silhouette.

The wardrobe department works under the designer's guidance. Everything must be tacked before it is machined, especially if the material has been cut on the cross. Stretchy fabrics are best sewn over a sheet of paper, as this reduces the pull on the stitching (the paper is subsequently removed). Accurate measurements and good linings are important, as is pressing them when they are finished, particularly if they are to be saved for future productions. Lining (especially for early period costumes) gives a fullness to geometrical shapes (for example, circles and half-circles) and is necessary when the inside of the costume is often visible. This is achieved by cutting the lining and the outer

material together, right sides facing each other. Tack and then machine them together, leaving an open slit to reverse the material when it is completed. Now iron it carefully. Hang it up overnight so that the fabric can find its own level. If necessary, adjust it and then sew up the slit.

Avoid jersey or stretchy fabrics and never use a flimsy lining fabric with very heavy material. Luckily for the designer and wardrobe department, the basic garments of earlier times were often designed so that there was a minimum of waste, yet they gave (with their variety of decoration) a look of comfort and richness.

Before studying the periods, the designer must be aware of the suitable use of shape. People's shapes reflect their personalities: plump, rounded shapes tend to indicate happy people while thin, narrow shapes can indicate meaner types. It is the designer's job to change the performer's shape to suit the character's physical outline. To achieve a plump outline, two T-shirts are needed, one larger than the other. On the smaller T-shirt, light-weight material or polyester wadding is built up to the required size. Each layer is pinned and glued. The whole is then covered with fine linen or muslin. The larger T-shirt is pulled over this and fixed with tacking stitches. This can then be put on and taken off with little or no trouble (Figure 2.1).

BIBLICAL AND EGYPTIAN

Biblical and Egyptian clothes are very simple in construction (see Figures 2.2–2.5). Their design follows three basic principles: social rank, occupation, and sexual attraction. Women's clothes tended to be seductive, particularly in Egyptian costume. Dress also shows personal or social rank, differentiating royalty, nobility, and lower classes. Other clothing was strictly utilitarian and was determined by the requirements of occupation or the need for protection against the rigours of the climate.

Colours were limited, especially in the brighter range, as most were made from

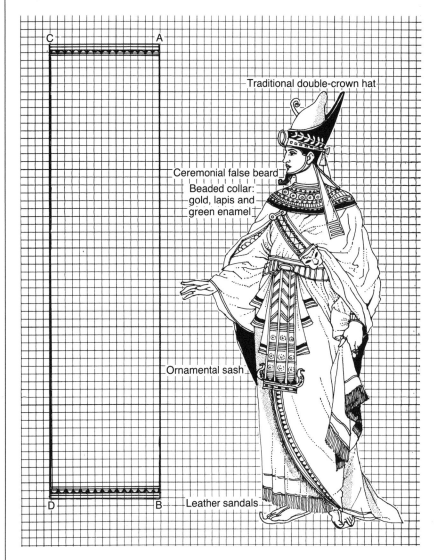

Traditional double-crown hat

Ceremonial false beard
Beaded collar:
gold, lapis and
green enamel

Ornamental sash

Leather sandals

Figure 2.2 Pattern for a Pharaoh. The material should be about 1.25 m wide and 4.5–5.5 m long for an average height. A cord should be tied round the waist. Hold corner A in front of the left side of the waist then throw the material upwards and over the right shoulder, allowing it to fall down the back. Take corner C and bring it round under the right arm and hold it together with corner A. Pull edge A–B (which is hanging over the right shoulder) downwards across the back to the left side of the waist. Bring it round to the front of the waist and pin it to corners A and C at the left side of the waist at the front, bringing the material to the front. Tuck in some pleats at the centre front into the waistcord, passing the material round to the right side of the waist; then upwards across the back over the left shoulder; down across the chest to the right side of the waist; pass a loop of material over the left hand; and then wrap a girdle around the waist over the entire robe, knotting it at the right side of the waist

mineral or vegetable dyes. The prevalence of indigo demonstrates that, for several centuries, this remained the most esteemed and widely used dye. At the time of the Pharaohs materials were mainly linen or wool, the latter often of a thick, coarse weave.

For over three thousand years, Egyptian dress style varied only gradually. The loin-cloth (or shenti) was basically a rectangular length of material wrapped around the body several times and kept in place either by tucking it in where it was tightly wrapped or by means of a girdle. Pharaohs' and priests' garments were chiefly of linen, often a fine, thin linen that was woven loosely to appear almost transparent.

A stiffened linen was also worn, which gave the appearance of being either goffered or pleated. This effect can be reproduced by using the same simple method as the Egyptians. A length of fine cotton material is placed into a bowl of very hot water, removed, and then twisted from either end. It is dipped occasionally back into the hot water and continuously twisted, until only a ball of cloth remains. All the water is then squeezed out and the ball of cloth is placed in a warm place. When fully dry, the ball is unwound, the material having been crimped into a series of wavy pleats.

Although there were simple colour schemes of red, blue, green, yellow, and deep purple, garments were usually bleached white. Decorations were mostly accessories, such as headdresses, bead collars, and girdles. Differences between the sexes were slight: high waisted for females while males were girded about the hips.

The kalasiris was common in this period and was worn by both men and women. It was made of transparent linen gauze, often with a design at its base, and it was worn over a loincloth. In its simplest form, this item of clothing consisted of a rectangular piece of material with an opening cut out of its centre, which allowed the head to be inserted through. The sides were sewn up leaving an opening for the arms. Sleeves were made separately and sewn on. These could be short and narrow, or long and wide. Kalasiris vary in width, being either full and wide or very close fitting. They could be full length or skirt length and were often worn with a girdle. The kalasiris of working people would be short and tucked up.

Figure 2.3 Egyptian queen's costume (the petticoat and cape costume). The garment consists of a straight piece of material threaded at the waist with a narrow strip of material or cord knotted at the front to keep the skirt in position. The cape material is oblong in shape. Take corners D and E and twist until triangles A–B–C and D–E–F have become narrow cords. Tie into a knot. Sew the skirt piece together at the narrow sides. A long girdle is placed around the waist and knotted at the back. The two ends are brought round to the front and knotted. The long ends are allowed to hang down. A deep ornamental collar is worn over the cape

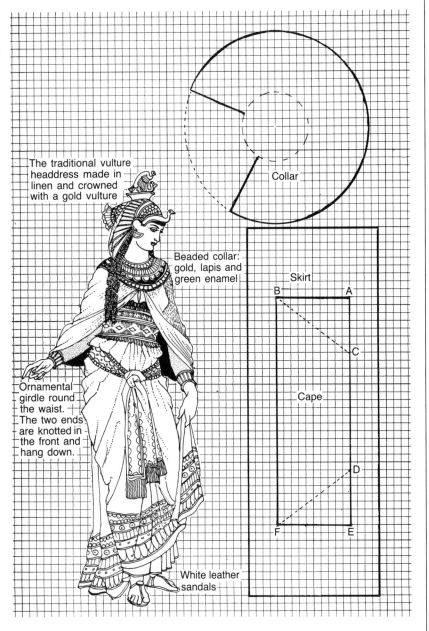

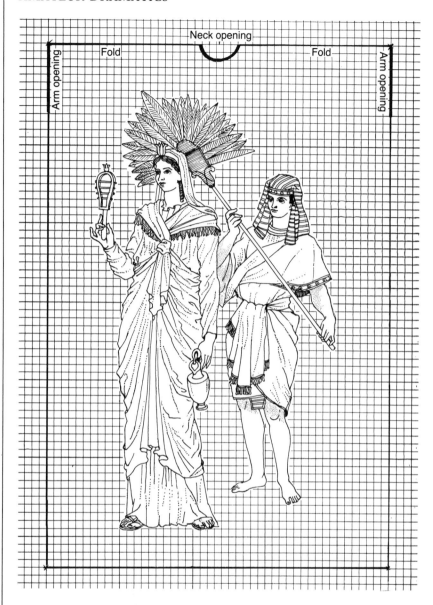

Figure 2.4 The kalasiris was made to be put on over the head. This garment consists of a piece of material the height of the wearer and wide enough to wrap around half again, with a piece over to tuck in at the top to keep it closed. This costume should be fairly tight fitting

A loose linen garment (not unlike a modern shirt) was worn by both Hebrew men and women. This tunic, the chethomene, was worn with a girdle around the waist, and it reached to ankle length. Its straight sleeves were either long or short. These tunics were fringed along their borders with tassels (called tsitsith). An over-tunic could be worn that was made in one piece. This had a length-ways slit running down over the head from the back to the chest, with slits at the sides for the arms. A hooded cloak was worn by higher ranks.

Thin gauze veils were worn by Jewish women. Turbans were worn by both sexes.

GREEK AND ROMAN

Classical Greek and Roman clothes were also very simple (see Figures 2.6–2.14). In Greece, clothing styles reflected the various architectural orders: straight lines with the Doric order, incurved lines with the Ionic order, and rich ornamentation with the Corinthian order.

The basic garment for a Greek women was the Doric peplos, which was made from a single rectangle of woven wool about 6 ft (2 m) wide and about 18 in (45 cm) more in height than the wearer as measured from shoulder to ankle. This was wrapped round the body and the excess fabric was folded over at the top. This was then pinned on both shoulders and the excess material was allowed to fall down, giving the effect of a short cape. It could be worn without a girdle, which left the side open, or it could be sewn from waist to hem. The excess material could then be tucked through a belt to be worn under the bust line, giving the effect of a blouse. A second belt could be used that gave the impression of two garments being worn. The design of this simple garment allowed for a variety of drapings and it permitted a number of different clothing styles without the need for cutting or sewing.

The peplos became the Ionic chiton, which was similar in style to the Doric but differed in the type of material used—now a thin linen or, occasionally, silk. Made from a single rectangle of fabric but wider than the Doric peplos, the chiton was about 10 ft (3 m) wide. It had no excess material and it measured exactly from shoulder to ankle. Because of its broad width,

Figure 2.5 Biblical costume for nativity plays, for example

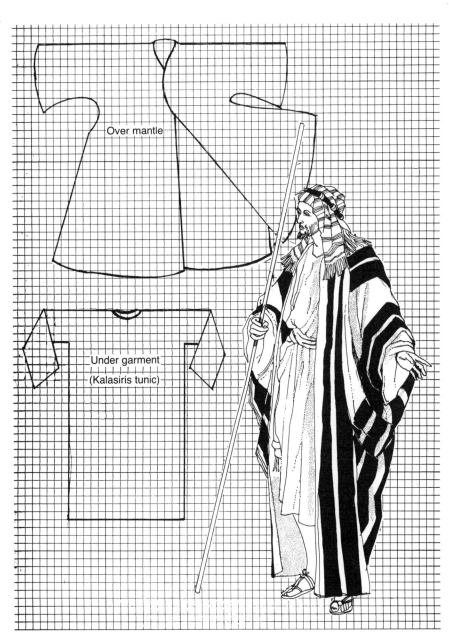

some eight to ten fibulae (clasps) were required to fasten the top edge. This left an open seam either side of the neck, which ran the length of the shoulders and down the arms to form an elbow-length sleeve. Being shorter than the Doric style, the chiton had no fullness or blousing effect, and it was girdled under the bust-line.

Men and women basically wore the same type of garment. There were also the short chiton, the himation (which was longer), and the chlamys—the cloak. All three garments consisted of simple, rectangular pieces of cloth, the only differences being their varied lengths and the draping and folding of the material. Sewing was used only occasionally: most garments were pinned together.

The Roman toga was also worn by both men and women, from the highest rank to the lowest plebian. The toga also remained in fashion until the fall of the Roman Empire. Because this garment could be used in biblical

Figure 2.6 The Doric peplos

Figure 2.7 The Ionic chiton

plays, Shakespearian plays, and many others, the designer should study it carefully. The toga was very large, being about three times the length of the wearer's body and twice his or her width. It had one straight side and the other was rounded off in a semi-circular fashion. It has been suggested that the toga was more intricate than this and was in fact made from various pieces of fabric that were then fastened together. However, there is no concrete evidence of this, but what is known is that the toga followed a set pattern with little or no variation. For the designer and the wardrobe department, the toga is not simple. Folds and drapes should be fixed into place to keep the costume in a controlled shape. To permit this, a simple shift should be made; the toga is then carefully folded and mounted onto this and then sewn down. This allows the performer greater freedom of movement.

The Roman tunic was really an imitation of the Greek chiton, and this too was worn by both sexes—halfway down the thigh for men and longer for women. The tunic was made of two pieces of material sewn together, which was put on over the head and pulled in at the waist by means of a girdle.

In this period, both Greek and Roman soldiers wore short chitons under their armour. The Greeks wore leather for protection, and the Romans metal breast-plates. Peasants also wore short chitons (but without the toga) as their only garment. When wide sleeves are attached to the short chiton it is called a dalmatica.

Senators wore their tunics edged with broad, purple borders. Knights wore a narrower

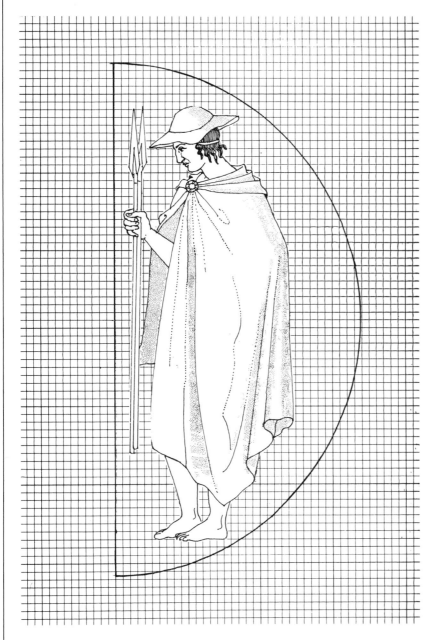

Figure 2.8 A Greek soldier wearing the chlamys, a travelling cloak fastened at the front with an ornamental brooch. He wears the petasos hat

Figure 2.9 *Opposite* The chiton and himation. Over the chiton is worn the himation, which is draped as follows. A corner is dropped over the body on the left side of the front to about calf length. The rest of the material is taken over the head and shoulders and brought over to the left shoulder, then draped over the left arm leaving the hand free. It is brought round the back and then placed over the right shoulder, encasing the arm and covering the hand. The drapery falls diagonally over the left hip. It is placed round the back and the folds are tucked into a girdle at the right of the waist. The rest is dropped down the right side. One end is raised to the left side of the waist and tucked in. The left hand can now hold the two parts of the drapery together at waist level

Figure 2.10 *Opposite right* A Greek soldier wearing a leather corselet covered with overlapping metal plates. The lower part of the body is protected by strips of leather. This is worn over the chiton. The helmet is of the Doric style

purple border. Roman women wore a long, straight tunic called a stola over their under-tunics, which fell to the feet. Over this was worn a voluminous cloak called a palla. This garment was rectangular in shape and was folded lengthways and held in place on each shoulder by a brooch or fibula.

For travelling, a Roman would wear a heavy woollen cape (paenula) with a hood (cucullus). Ordinary people wore a hooded cape made from coarse brown wool (bacroocullus). For

Greek, Roman, Assyrian, and Persian costumes, use flannelette, heavy cheese-cloth, furnishing fabrics, muslin, rayon crêpe, and unbleached calico.

POST-ROMAN AND BYZANTINE

In the post-Roman Byzantine period, clothing remained simple. Roman styles persisted, and the popular garment was the long undershirt—

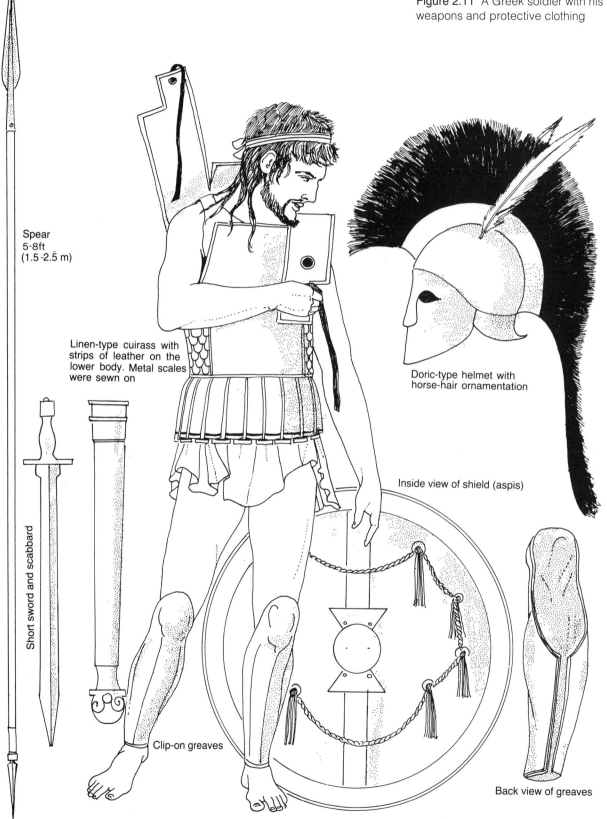

Figure 2.11 A Greek soldier with his weapons and protective clothing

Spear
5-8ft
(1.5-2.5 m)

Linen-type cuirass with strips of leather on the lower body. Metal scales were sewn on

Doric-type helmet with horse-hair ornamentation

Short sword and scabbard

Inside view of shield (aspis)

Clip-on greaves

Back view of greaves

42

Figure 2.12 The Roman toga. The main feature of this garment is its size: the length is three times the height of the wearer and twice the wearer's height in width. It is put on by folding it lengthwise about the middle in broad folds. It is then hung over the left shoulder, leaving about a third in length hanging in front. The remainder is passed diagonally across the back, under the right arm, and thrown back over the left shoulder. Because of its width, it covers the left arm. The part crossing the back is spread out to cover the right shoulder blade. The corner that hangs forward over the left shoulder is made shorter by drawing the toga up at the chest and letting it fall over the folds. These folds at the chest served as a pocket (the sinus)

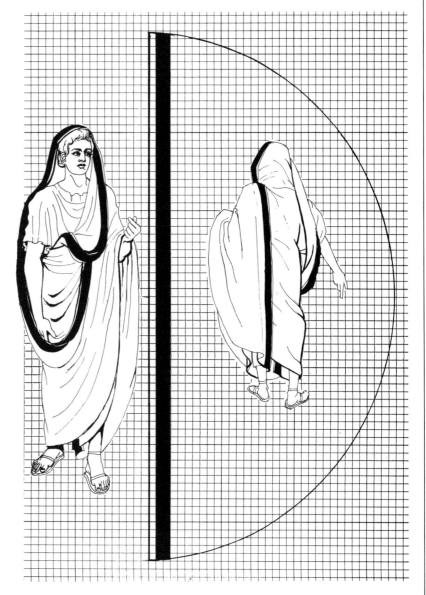

a straight garment with long, tight sleeves. The overtunic was similar to the Roman tunica—the sleeves were open (simply holes) and its length varied from just below the knee to just over the foot. Reminiscent of Roman legionaries, legs were covered in breeches or braccae. Early in the period, the dalmatica tunic was commonly worn but later it was only worn by high dignitaries and priests, when it became a richly embroidered mantle.

The cloak now assumed an essential part of dress, and it was worn indoors as well as out. In its simplest form, it was a rectangular piece of material worn round the shoulders, which fell to the ground and was fastened on the right shoulder with a brooch. For formal wear, a semi-circular cape was worn. This, too, was fastened on the right shoulder with an ornamental brooch. Fitted with a detachable hood, this cape was sewn up at the front with a slit for the head. Ordinary workers are shown wearing breeches tucked in to knee-length boots, with thigh-length loose-sleeved tunics and ankle-length cloaks.

Women's clothing was similar to men's— long, high-necked, straight tunics reaching the

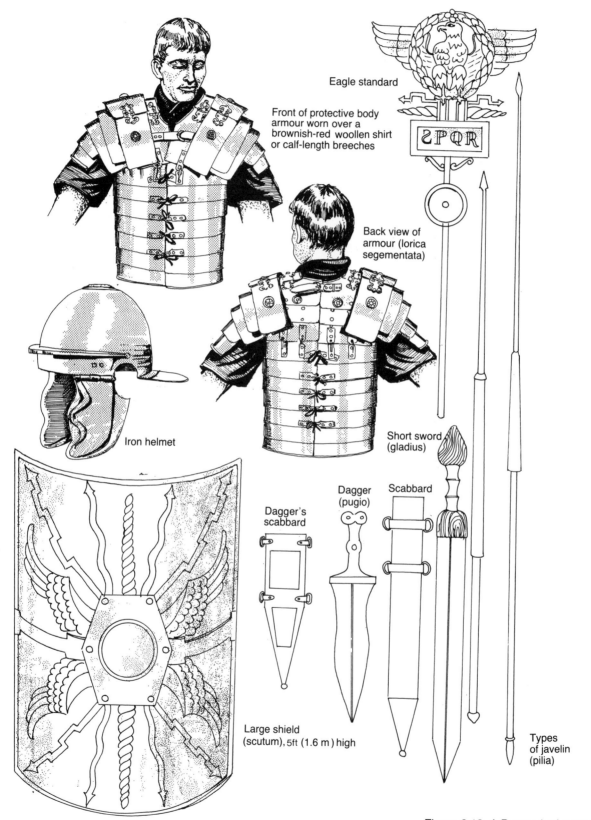

Eagle standard

Front of protective body armour worn over a brownish-red woollen shirt or calf-length breeches

Back view of armour (lorica segementata)

Iron helmet

Short sword (gladius)

Dagger (pugio)

Scabbard

Dagger's scabbard

Large shield (scutum), 5ft (1.6 m) high

Types of javelin (pilia)

Figure 2.13 A Roman legionary with his armour and weapons

Figure 2.14 A Roman general (later to become the dress of the emperor in the *toga picta*). This is made and dressed as the toga in Figure 2.12. The hem is stencilled in a purple colour

ankle, with long sleeves, and drawn in at the waist by a girdle. Over this was worn a further tunic, slightly shorter, that could also be girdled. A veil was worn, draped over the forearm. Similar to men, women wore cloaks and capes. Their hairstyles remained the same as the Imperial Roman style—very elaborate and often held in place under a turban. Working women coiled their hair on their heads and covered it with modest veils or hoods.

ANGLO-SAXON TO NORMAN

For the costume designer of this period, information is scarce. This is the time of the Dark Ages, and what evidence there is for the early part of this period comes from discoveries of garments in the peat bogs of north-west Germany, Denmark, and Holland (see Figures 2.15–2.17).

Men wore shirt-like smocks or tunics with or without sleeves. These were made from hide, leather, or patterned woollen material. These tunics had an opening at the chest and were knee length; they slipped over the head or were sewn on one shoulder, the other being fastened with a brooch or clasp. Under this tunic, short breeches with leg bandages of wool, hide strips bound round the knee and shins, or ankle-length, cross-gartered breeches were worn. Cloaks were as earlier: semi-circular or rectangular in shape with hoods.

Women wore long shirts with running draw-strings, over which a tunic was worn similar to the men's sleeveless shirt smocks. Women also wore cloaks like the men's.

With the intermingling of the Teutonic people and the Roman–Byzantine civilizations, a gradual change in fashion and material took place. A garment worn by men and women alike (though varying in length and the amount of fabric used) was the bliaut. This was a close-fitting tunic that was either laced or sewn up on one or both sides. Sleeves (open beneath the elbow) revealed the close sleeve of the under-tunic. The bliaut's skirt varied in length from knee to ankle, and was sometimes slit at the sides or front and back. Men often wore this garment to just below the knee, and the skirt was belted at the waist and bloused over the

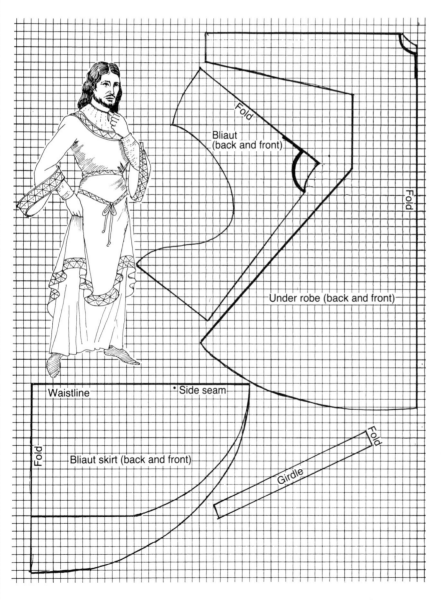

Figure 2.15 The bliaut fashion

Figure 2.16 Anglo-Saxon and Norman men's clothing

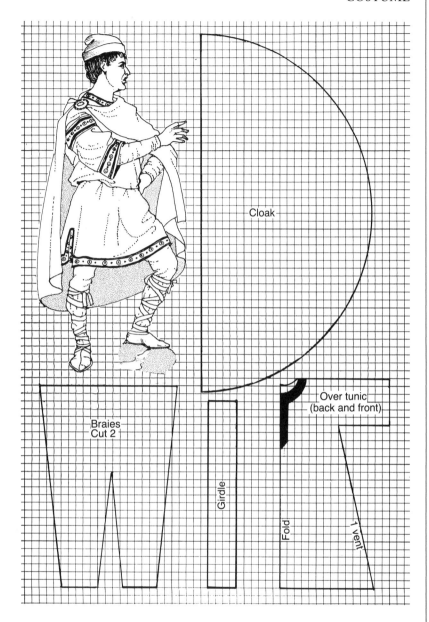

stomach to conceal the belt. Men wore short breeches hidden under this long tunic, or sometimes long breeches with or without cross-gartering.

The upper classes wore tailor-made stockings, but peasants wore coarse, heavy stockings that often appear clumsy and wrinkled. Outer garments at this time remained basically the same as earlier: cloaks—rectangular, semi-circular, or circular—fastened on either the left or right shoulder by a brooch.

Women wore a long undertunic that followed the overgarment's close or loose fitting. This linen chemise was long—to the ground—and had a close, high neckline and long, close sleeves. Over the chemise was worn the shorter, looser garment (bliaut), which had short, wide sleeves that revealed the chemise's sleeves at the wrists. Being close fitting, the bliaut was tightly laced to create the then-fashionable small waistline. The court-dress bliaut was made of a heavy jersey-type material, which also fitted closely to the figure. Its skirt was made from a finer fabric, which fell in small pleats to the

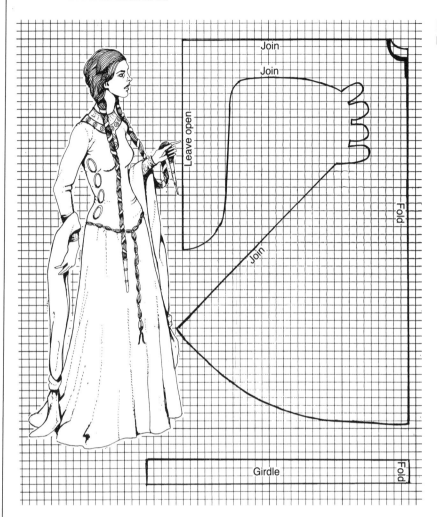

Figure 2.17 Anglo-Saxon and Norman women's clothing

ground. This garment was made from a great amount of fabric and was sometimes slit up each side; the bulk of the fabric was allowed to form a train. The front could be tied into a knot, which revealed the legs. These were covered in loose stockings. A further exaggeration (which gives the designer further scope) was to use so much material in the sleeves and veils that very large knots had to be tied in them to prevent them from trailing on the ground. The girdle (which encircled the waist) was made of gold or silver cord, coloured wool, strips of pleated leather, cloth, or strung metal discs. The waistline was variable but normally just above or below the hips.

Because many stage characters are clerics, a brief description of their clothing is included. A monk's main garment is the habit, which consists of a long, plain white tunic that reaches the ground. Over this was worn a loose, black, full gown, with an attached hood. The monk's head was shaven and, as no performer will submit to such a drastic haircut, a wig must be purchased or hired. The ecclesiastical robes of a bishop changed little in this period: a long, white tunic (or alb) with loose sleeves and a band of embroidery around the bottom. A scarf-length piece of material or stole was embroidered at the ends and had deep fringing. A woven, linen girdle cord was tied around the alb's waist, and a white, linen, embroidered separate collar was tied on with tape. A three-quarter circle (or chasuble) was placed over the alb and this hung down in deep folds. The dalmatica (shaped like a cross without seams) was also placed over the head, with a slit for the neck opening. The cope was a full semi-circle of richly decorated fabric, to ground length, that was worn fastened across the chest with clasps. A bishop's headgear was a low, mitre hat. The colours of the different monastic orders are Benedictine (black), Dominican (black over a white robe), Carmelite (brown and white), Carthusian (white), and Franciscan (brown).

MEDIEVAL

Early medieval clothing (Figures 2.19–21)—cut on geometric lines—made no attempt to fit the figure accurately. The basic garment of this period was made very simply: worn by all men was the chemise—a loose type of shirt that varied in length from mid-thigh to calf. The neckline was a simple round slit cut at the throat. Peasants wore a shorter version of this, often with the chemise's tails tucked into a belt.

Higher-class men wore a variety of over-

Figure 2.18 Ecclesiastical clothes

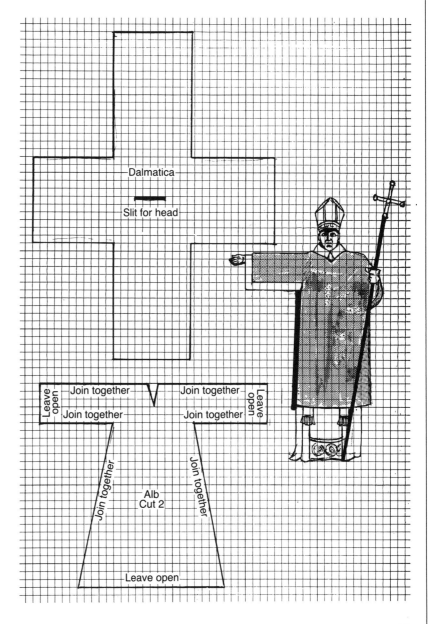

Dalmatica

Slit for head

Leave open

Join together   Join together

Join together   Join together

Leave open

Join together

Join together

Alb
Cut 2

Leave open

garments. The cote (a long, skirted tunic) fell to below the knee or to the ankle, and this had sleeves and a body that was cut in one piece that gave a loose, flowing effect. There was a wide neckline below the collar bone, and narrow, close-fitting sleeves that buttoned on the outside from the elbow to a tight-fitting cuff. The cote was belted above the hips and, to give fullness, it hung a little over the belt. The commonest outer garment was the surcote: a sleeveless tunic, looser and wider than the cote and that fell to either the knee or ankle. Slit in the back or occasionally in the front, this had tails that were tucked in to the belt. The neckline was a slit at the throat, and a hood could be attached here. These three garments—chemise, cote, and surcote—made the basic clothing for a man of this period. Research in the manuscript departments of museum, effigies on tombs, and brasses are all good sources of information to give an authentic look to stage costumes.

After the thirteenth century, clothes became more close fitting, following the lines of the body, and with less fullness in the skirts. This produced a more slender, elegant silhouette. The cotehardie was a high-waisted garment with a single skirt. It was short sleeved and often had tippets—long pieces of fabric hanging down from the elbow. This was knee length and had a shallow, wide neckline that was lower than the cote's. This was invariably worn with a chaperon—a hooded shoulder cape that extended from the neck to the upper chest and arms. The body and skirt were joined, and the seam was covered with a belt. A gipon (a quilted, waist-length doublet) was worn under the cotehardie but showed only from elbow to wrist. The focus of attention at this time was the silhouette: extra padding accentuated the narrow waistline look.

Another development was the herygaud—a voluminous garment that fell in folds to the knee or ankle. This had wide sleeves that extended well beyond the hands. The sleeves had long, vertical slits at about elbow level; the rest of the sleeve from elbow to wrist would then hang loose below the arm. This garment was hooded and did not have a belt.

The tabard style of overgarment was also worn. Under this, close-fitting drawers (of bulky hose to knee or ankle length) were worn, which were hidden by the chemise or exposed when the tails were tucked into the belt. If these breeches-like drawers were long they were gartered at the knee or, when short, knotted above the knee, the calves being left bare. The nobility wore well-fitting hose beneath their tunics. These were separately seamed stockings attached with straps or brooches to the belt of the underwear.

The popularity of long hose gradually led to the shortening of underdrawers: one-piece hose with a parti-coloured pattern were making their appearance. Parti-coloured hose (usually one striped and the other plain) belonged to a king's or a nobleman's household (the designer could well incorporate modern tights for this period). Outer garments consisted of mantles and capes, which were long and circular or semi-circular and slit entirely up the front. They were fastened on the right shoulder or at the throat. A variety of hoods was worn, either with or without a cape or cloak.

Women's clothes resembled the men's in many ways, although they were longer. As with men, the basic female garment was the chemise but, for a woman, this was a long, high-necked undershirt that reached down to the instep and it had long, close-fitting sleeves.

For the lower classes, the chemise was often the only indoor garment. Over this chemise was worn the cote or kirtle—a loose-fitting gown with long sleeves that could also be loose and cut in one with the body, or tight and often laced. The fullness of the garment's body was gathered in at the waist, belted above the hips, and the belt's tongue was allowed to hang down to the knees. The neckline was slit a little down the front, and this was fastened with either a brooch or lacing. A short, U-neck opening was also worn. Fitchets or pocket slits, cut in at the front, gave access to a purse that was worn underneath.

Rank manifests itself only in the quality of material. A simple cote or chemise was the

Figure 2.19 Chaperon and liripipe hoods

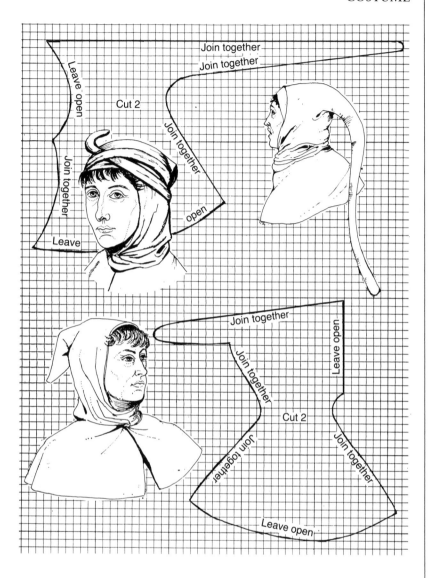

typical dress of peasant women, and these were often cut shorter or tucked up into a girdle for ease of movement. The surcote was a long garment with voluminous folds and a wide back. This was generally close fitting at the waist and hips than that worn by men. In the early part of the period sleeves were wide and capacious but later became tighter fitting, often with buttoned sleeves that, like the men's style, were left open to fall from the elbow. As all these styles changed slowly the designer can incorporate most of them without losing historical accuracy. In the sleeveless surcotes the armholes became long slits that revealed a contrasting cote beneath. It is essential to remember (when costuming women for this period) the importance of combining such garments as cote and surcote with contrasting colours—with patches of undergarment showing at the neck, sides, and cuff. The neck opening of the surcote was wide, and it extended to both shoulders. A knee-length surcote with a deep, jagged hem that contrasted strongly with a long cote worn underneath was very popular at this time. For dagging use a rayon jersey as this needs no hemming. When costuming queens or noble women, dress them in very plain, unbelted gowns instead of the surcote. These gowns had flowing folds of rich material, with a single brooch fastening at the neck. Top garments for outdoor wear were the cloak or mantle—long and fully circular or semi-circular, with or without a hood fastened at the neck with a clasp, brooch, or cord. Although women wore hose these were never seen because of their long gowns.

The fifteenth century brought in an exaggeration in clothing, and many types of novelty garments made their appearance. For men, the chemise remained the basic garment: long sleeved and thigh length. Over this was worn a doublet that was normally sleeved and fastened either at the front or back, padded or quilted, and tailored close to the body. A straight, hip-length skirt was attached to this doublet at the waist. This was worn with a thigh-length gown similar to the cotehardie that was belted at the waist and had full sleeves, giving in silhouette a broad chest and a slim waist. The principal long gown, the houppelande, was very popular. This was tailored to give a more stylish fit. A flowing, floor-length gown, the houppelande was slit to thigh to ease walking. It was made of four pieces of fabric seamed at the front, back, and sides, and fastened down the front either with buttons or hooks-and-eyes concealed in a front fold. The sleeves were large and open and often had large trailing cuffs that hung to the ground. The collar was high, extending to the back of the head, and fastened at the front, which had a V-shaped opening. Other collars were worn—a flat, turned-down collar or even no collar at all—all were popular. Men's hose became longer, reaching to

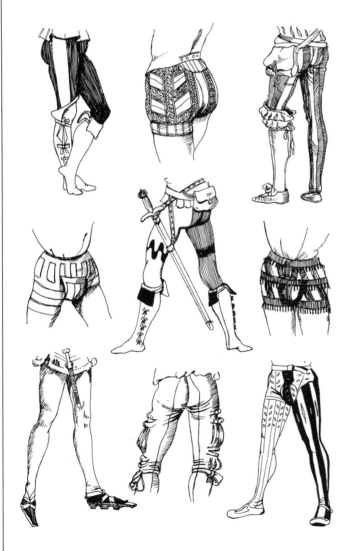

Figure 2.20 Parti-coloured hose styles

Figure 2.21 The female houppelande fashion of the fifteenth century

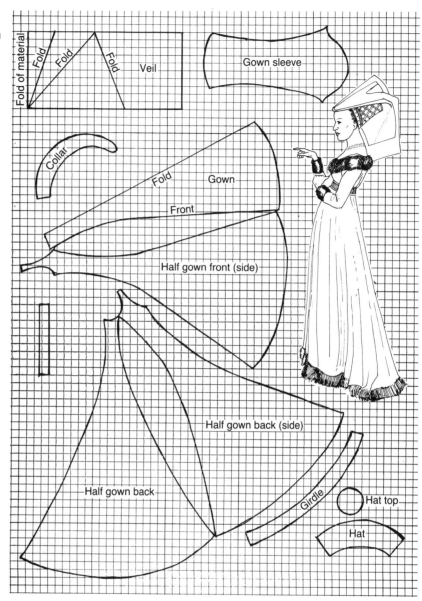

the crotch, where it was attached with laces to the doublet. Hose was made in one with a cod-piece.

For women, the chemise remained the basic undergarment but now with the popular *décolletée* neckline. Although the cotehardie remained in fashion, a new corset-style of garment came in. This was laced at the front and had short sleeves to reveal the chemise sleeves underneath. Also fashionable was the sleeveless surcote cut away at the sides to give large armholes from armpit to hip and leaving only a strip of fabric (usually fur trimmed) at the front and back. This garment's wide, open neckline gave the effect of shoulder straps, and the bodice extended down to a broad hipband from which the full skirt fell. The front of the bodice was decorated with rows of buttons, from neck to hip. The surcote's bodice extended so far below the waist that the open sides revealed the hip belt and the contrasting colours of the cote beneath. In later styles the hipband dipped in a U-shape over the stomach. As with all over-dresses and gowns, the surcote's skirts should be richly lined in order to create the maximum effect when they are gathered or held up for walking.

For outer garments, women effected the male type of houppelande, which was always long (to the ground) and tailored and unbelted, or girded to a high waistline and pleated down to a full skirt. Sleeves, like the men's, varied from capacious wide funnels, long hanging sleeves, baggy sleeves gathered at the shoulders and cuffs, or simply narrow and close fitting to the cuff. Necklines varied, being either high, stand-up necklines, V-throated, or they assumed a decanter-mouth style that curled away from the head at ear level. The flat, turned-down collar was also popular, and this was combined with a very deep *décolletage* to reveal the bodice and possibly also the chemise. At ceremonies, circular mantles were worn off the shoulder. These hung in a train from the neck by means of jewelled cords.

RENAISSANCE

At the Renaissance, the doublet (a shorter style of tunic like a waistcoat) was worn over the chemise. This had no skirts and fastened down the back. Necklines were flat and cut low to the collar bone, or they plunged in a U-shape to the waist. Sleeves were usually tied into the armholes with points and, through the gaps, the chemise would be seen. Alternatively, the body and sleeves could be cut in one. Sleeve styles included the straight, close-fitting type or the baggy and wrinkled type that was pleated into a snug fit at the wrist. The front and sleeves of the doublet might be slashed to reveal the chemise cloth or a contrasting lining that was puckered through the slits. The essential feature of the doublet was its silhouette—a narrow, close-fitting waist that accentuated the wearer's broad shoulders. This is the look that became established for men's clothing throughout the Renaissance. Over the doublet was worn a jerkin, which was open at the front to reveal the doublet. The jerkin's skirt extended to the hips or, more popularly, to the knee. Necklines

varied from high collars with wider revers to low, square or round necks. The older style of hanging sleeves with vertical arm slits at the elbows was adapted to the jerkin. Jerkin sleeves were made large to accommodate the doublet's bulky sleeves. These could be short, elbow length, very padded, or extended down the arm to the wrist and again extensively padded. Hose were now split into two parts, the upper and nether stocks. Upper stocks were breeches-like garments that could vary in length from short to knee length and be either close fitting or puffed out and slashed, and decorated in boldly contrasting colours (see Figures 2.22–23).

The woman's silhouette also changed during this period: a tighter-waisted effect came into fashion. Women wore close-fitting bodices and voluminous skirts that trailed around their feet and on the ground. The new fashion also included a tight, front-laced bodice that was worn over an underdress that could be seen through the lacing. This bodice was fitted to the skirts either at the waist or at the hips, or the front panel might dip in a deep U-shape over the stomach. The gown was belted with a wide-linked or woven braided girdle. Skirts were long and trailing but not open at the front—they were probably lifted to show the contrasting skirt underneath. Close-fitting sleeves were tied to the armholes to reveal in the gap the chemise beneath. A decorative slit might be made the length of the sleeve at the back, and this was laced at intervals. Also, a wide-mouthed full-length sleeve or a more moderate elbow sleeve were worn.

The female silhouette later became square, with a broad square or round *décolletage* at the back as well as the front. Gowns were usually cut in large circles with the result that waists were considerably smaller in circumference than hems, which trailed on the ground in massed folds. To walk unencumbered, women held the bulk of the gown's fabric gathered up over their stomachs. A style of separate bodice and skirt also developed. Bodices were back laced, and these lay flat over the chest with a low, square, *décolletage*. Skirts were full and pleated in heavy layers to give a bell shape to

Figure 2.22 The use of tights and jerkins for a Shakespearian play

the lower silhouette.

Clothing typical of a peasant was a simple cote with long, moderate, turned-back sleeves that showed the close-fitting chemise sleeves. Peasant women wore a front-laced bodice.

THE SIXTEENTH CENTURY

In the sixteenth century, the Spanish influence was very prominent. For men, the doublet was now close fitting with a short skirt. It was tight waisted and was pointed at the front, which overhung the girdle. The neckline had a standing collar with stiffened tabs that stood out at right angles. These tabs, or piccadills, were used to support the earlier, small, neck ruffs. Later the collar became high at the back and low at the front to accommodate the larger ruffs. The doublet was fastened by buttons and loops from collar to waist. The doublet's body was stiffened with buckram and well padded with wool or horsehair. Skirts were now so short they were almost hidden by the girdle but were flared out to cover the join between the doublet and the stuffed hose. Double skirts were not uncommon. Sleeves were made either narrow and close fitting to the wrist (and fastened with buttons) or else in the leg-o'-mutton shape known as 'trunk' sleeves, which were pinked and slashed and worn with false, hanging sleeves. The girdle, made from leather, velvet, or silk, supported hangers for swords and daggers.

The jerkin was unpadded and worn over the doublet with a high or low collar. It was fashionable to wear one's arm in one sleeve only—the other hanging loosely. Cloaks and capes were of various lengths, from short to ankle length.

The fashionable silhouette was the ruff. The small ruff (attached to the chemise or separate) was often worn open at the throat; the medium-sized ruff was closed all round; and the cartwheel or large ruff was also closed all round. Wire frameworks were used to support the larger one. (See Figure 2.24 for a figure-of-eight ruff pattern.)

Trunk hose was the popular garment of this period; this was padded and covered the thighs and was in one with the stockings. Later the term hose came to refer only to the breeches.

Both styles were slashed and, from the slashings, a contrasting colour was visible. Canions (or leg coverings) filled the space between trunk hose and stockings. Breeches (or hose with separate stockings) were made in various styles. Some fastened just below the knee and were either skin tight with the stockings pulled up over them and gartered above the knee or were gathered in at the waist and padded round the hips.

Women wore a corseted bodice that was very rigid and stiffened with whalebone stays. The

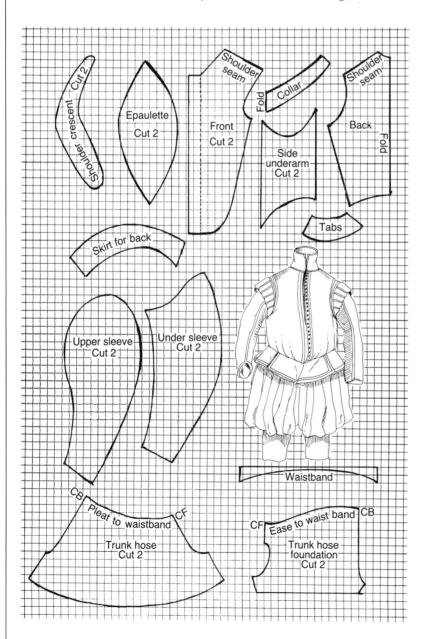

Figure 2.23 The doublet and trunkhose fashion

Figure 2.24 The figure-of-eight ruff

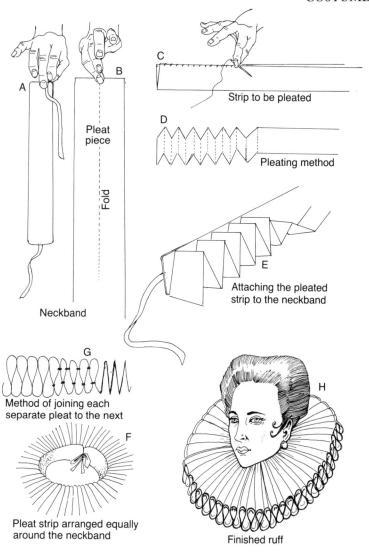

A

B

Pleat
piece

Fold

Neckband

C

Strip to be pleated

D

Pleating method

E

Attaching the pleated
strip to the neckband

G

Method of joining each
separate pleat to the next

F

Pleat strip arranged equally
around the neckband

H

Finished ruff

waist was low and deeply pointed at the front, often having a scallop edge. The neckline (which was either low or high) was cut square if worn low and arched slightly over the bosom. This low *décolletage* was covered either by a high-necked chemise with a standing collar and a small, open frill at the throat, or just ornamental jewellery. The high neckline had a standing collar with a small Medici collar within. A closed, cartwheel-type ruff was usually worn. The cuffs matched the collar and were made of lawn, cambric, or lace. Sleeves were close fitting to the wrist, slightly padded, puffed, and slashed, and finished with either a hand cuff or a turned-back cuff. Sleeves were slashed, had roll wings (either double, single, or even a large plain roll, which hid the stitching at the join), or had hanging sleeves that later became simply sham sleeves.

The long skirts of the wealthier classes were encrusted with precious metals and gem stones and were worn open to reveal the rich under-gown or petticoat of the same length underneath. This skirt was conical in shape and was called the Spanish farthingale. It consisted of an undergown that spread out straight from the waist with circular wooden, steel, or whalebone hoops. The shape varied from being tunnel-shaped, bell-shaped, or dome-shaped, and it was made from canvas, buckram, or heavy linen. The overskirt was made to stand stiffly outwards from the waist to the ground, making its surface smooth without draperies or folds.

The French farthingale (which came in a little later) was in two styles: the roll farthingale (known affectionately as the bum roll) was a padded bolster roll worn round the hips that tilted slightly up at the back and was tied with tapes at the front; the wheel farthingale (or Catherine wheel) was a wheel-shaped structure made from steel or whalebone that was worn round the waist and that tilted forward, was raised at the back, and down at the front. In silhouette it looked like a large bustle. The skirt was made full enough to be carried out at right angles and to fall over the farthingale and then vertically to the feet.

The gown that was worn over this bodice and skirt was loose bodied with fitted shoulders. It fell in folds to give an inverted V-shape. It also opened at the front to reveal the dress beneath. Having a standing collar that was open at the throat with ties going down, this gown could be closed from neck to hem. Its sleeves were short and puffed out, with a kick-up effect at the shoulders. The sleeves ended just above the elbow.

THE SEVENTEENTH CENTURY

This period had two influences: the old Spanish style and the new French and Dutch styles. The older Spanish-style of clothing for women was the bodice and petticoat. The gown remained separate, and could be worn with or without a farthingale. Low-neckline bodices stayed in fashion, with the long, tapering waists edged with a narrow, doublet skirt of scalloped tabs. The fastenings down the front were hidden by a stomacher, which gave an extreme *décolletage* cut below the bosom. This was the fashion for unmarried women.

The high-necked bodice was also worn without the stomacher. This was then fastened down the front with buttons or lacing, and fastened at the neck with a closed ruff. The trunk sleeves were full at the top, with a kick-up effect at the shoulder, then they narrowed towards the wrist where they were fastened with buttons and finished with hand cuffs. Large, hanging sleeves (usually false) were sometimes added. Close-fitting sleeves were worn open at the seam and fastened by a ribbon at the elbow, which revealed the partlet sleeve below.

The doublet—a type of bodice without padding and that was close fitting and flared from the waist—was collarless. This was cut to a wide V- or U-shape at the front, sometimes revealing the bosom. Sleeves were close fitting, fastening at the wrist with buttons and lace cuffs. Shoulders were always fitted with wings. The type of skirt depended on the type of the nether garments worn and, whether it was a farthingale or petticoats, it was ankle length.

From about 1625 the ruff and the farthingale began to disappear. The bodice now became short waisted and was given a higher waistline effect with or without a basque. Basqued bodices were similar to the male doublet, with square, deep tabs. Bodices had both front and back fastenings but were most often laced at the back. The neckline was a very low *décolletage*, and was either square or round. The basqueless bodice fitted tightly to the waist, which came to a point at the front and was stiffened with whalebone. Both garments had a narrow sash or belt that followed the waistline and was tied in a bow. Sleeves were full and paned below and above the elbow, finishing at the wrist with cuffs that matched the now-drooping collar. The skirt was loosely gathered at the waist and was soft, falling in irregular folds to the ground. The elongated, inverted, V-opening at the front revealed the petticoat, which was often of the same fabric and colour as the skirt (the closed skirt became more popular later). In fashion for the whole of this century was the nightgown or négligé. This was worn during the day for formal and informal functions and was a gown without a stiffened underbodice. Although ruffs can be included in costume designs, the clothing of this period can be combined with later styles, for example, the 'broad Bertha'—a wide collar that reached from neck to shoulder. Hand ruffs went out of fashion as the turned-back cuff became more fashionable. Long cloaks that reached the ground and had large, turned-down collars, were mainly worn for travelling. The short cape or tippet, which ended just below the waist, was also popular.

For men, the doublet now had longer tabs, which curved down at the front to a point to create a long-waisted effect. This usually had a belly piece. The waistline was studded with eyelets for attaching the breeches by means of lace ties. The doublet was fastened from the top of the high-standing collar to the waist with buttons and loops. Plain and close-fitting sleeves were sometimes full at the top and paned at the shoulders and elbows, and fastened with buttons to the wrist. The panes revealed the coloured lining. Wings encircled the shoulder joins.

In designing for plays of the mid-century, the designer can mix styles: the doublet had now become looser fitting and high waisted. Gone was the padding; there was little or no stiffening. The corseted silhouette had gone out of fashion and the doublet had virtually become a waistcoat with sleeves. The doublet was sometimes so short that a gap was created between doublet and breeches. This was bridged by a protruding shirt. Shirts were now full and loose in both body and sleeve. Collars were usually stiffened with buckram, which also supported the upright band of the standing or falling collar.

A popular garment of this period was the leather jerkin. This was of military origin. It was close fitting and had a high waistline and deep skirt that overlapped at the front, and was slit at the back and sides. It had a collarless, round neck and was buttoned down the front to the waist. It could be worn with or without sleeves or with tubular, hanging sleeves. The cassock coat was also popular. This was wide and flared loosely out towards the hem. It was fastened down the front with buttons and ribbons and usually had a rounded, collarless neckline.

Falling, large-band neckwear became very popular. Neck pieces were tied at the front with white band, strings, or tasselled cords. A length of folded linen was also tied loosely round the neck, its ends being decorated with lace. This was known as the cravat.

Breeches were very full, unpadded, and baggy at the knee. They could also be full at the top and moderately tight over the knees, being buttoned and decorated with bunches of ribbon loops.

For women of the mid-seventeenth century, the boned and close-fitting bodice was again long waisted, coming to a deep point at the front. A horizontal, low-cut neckline encircled the bosom and bared the shoulders. This neckline was edged by the chemise's lace and below by a deep, lace bertha. Stomachers continued to be worn, and these were ornamented by arrangements of ribbon loops down their centres. Sleeves varied from being full to the elbow and gathered into a band from which emerged the full, frilled sleeve of the chemise, to being short and straight and ending just above the elbow, where they were trimmed at the lower edge with lace or ribbon loops.

The skirt was gathered at the waist and hung loosely to the ground. The front was usually open to reveal the petticoat underneath. The front edges of the skirt were either folded back and secured or allowed to fall naturally to the ground. A bustle was worn, and the overskirt was gathered up behind.

The gown's bodice was close fitting and joined to a fully gathered trained skirt, which was open at the front. The neckline was either square or round and was edged with a border that came over the shoulders to form a V-shape at the waist, where it was tied with a ribbon or girdle. The gap so created was filled with an embroidered stomacher. Sleeves were usually short, plain, and straight, ending just above the elbow. The frilled sleeve of the chemise hung below. Later, single or multiple frills were attached. The petticoat was slightly shorter than the gown and was sometimes trained in various patterns of flounces, fringes, embroidery, and quilting.

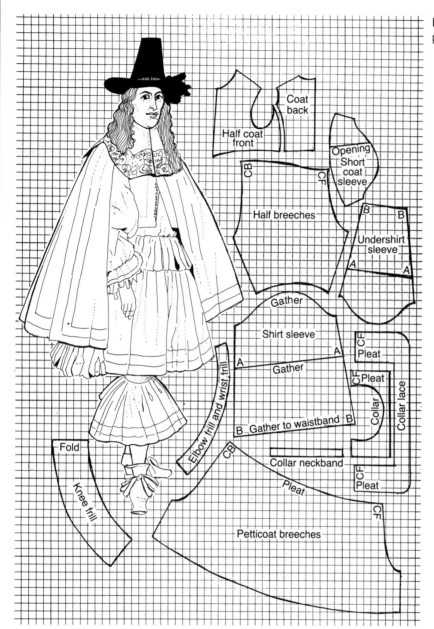

Figure 2.25 The Rhinegrave or petticoat fashion

The mantua, although similar to the gown, was looser and was used mainly as a wrap. Made of silk, it was always black or a dark colour. Coats were similar to men's and were worn for walking or horse riding. The waist-length tippet was also fashionable. This was usually double, the upper cape forming a deep collar of velvet or fur. Large scarves, shoulder deep and falling almost to the knee, were similarly very fashionable.

The man's silhouette at this period was still the short doublet with skirt, but the doublet was longer and more closely fitting and the skirt was plain. From the middle of the seventeenth century, the doublet was replaced by the coat and the waistcoat. Waistcoats were close fitting at the waist and collarless; skirts fell loosely to just below the knee and were fastened at the waist by a sash. Sleeves were short and loose fitting. The surcoat (a loose coat with short sleeves) was worn over the waistcoat. This was shorter and was fastened at the top by a clasp. The surcoat fitted at the shoulders and hung loosely down to just below the knee. The skirt had side slits or vents to the hips.

The surcoat was collarless and was fastened from neck to hem with buttons but was usually worn open. Large, horizontal pockets were positioned very low on the skirt, some 2–3 in (5–8 cm) from the hem. Sleeves were cut to elbow length and ended in deep, turned-back cuffs that were fastened to the sleeve by buttons. Later, the coat's cut became closer fitting and the pockets were positioned higher up the skirt. Sleeves also became longer, almost reaching the wrist. The shoulder knot's trimmings (a bunch of ribbon loops) were only worn on the right shoulder.

By the end of the century the coat had become close fitting and a definite waistline effect had been created as the skirt had become fuller and flared out. The waistcoat had become a little shorter and was fastened by a few buttons to the waist. The remaining buttonholes were merely decorative. The openings so left revealed the frilled shirt and cravat. The outdoor garment was now the overcoat—the Brandenburg—a large, loose-fitting coat that was shapeless and came to calf length.

During this period, men also wore nightgowns and turbans as négligé. This became informal dress, and was initially long, loose, and made of cotton. Later, heavy brocades or silk with contrasting linings became more fashionable. The turban or nightcap was worn when a man removed his wig. When the coat had short sleeves, shirt sleeves were full and ended at the wrist in a full frill or ruffle. Breeches were wide and these remained in vogue until about 1670.

Most fashionable (but mainly at court) were the Rhinegraves or petticoat pantaloons (see Figure 2.25). The silhouette was now a very wide leg reaching the knee, fastened at the waistband, and pleated—which resembled a short, divided skirt. This was lavishly ornamented with lace and ribbon loops: ribbon loops formed a fringe round the waist and deep

cannons of lace hung down the knees.

For ordinary fashionable men, plain, knee-length, close-fitting breeches (generally of a different material from the coat) were worn, which were fastened at the outer side of the knee with buttons or buckles.

THE EIGHTEENTH CENTURY

(See Figures 2.26–29.) The early part of the eighteenth century was theatrical in its sense of colour, possibly because, under Louis XIV, fabrics were garish and most European countries followed French fashion. The costume designer must try to recreate and, if possible, emphasize this. After Louis' death in 1715, colours became invariably harmonious, soft, and subtle, and harsh colours were avoided. This is a century famous for its brocades, silks, chintz, and painted calico.

At the start of the century women wore a gown and a petticoat and the bodice and skirt were joined. This was an open-robe style: the gown was open at the front to reveal the petticoat, which was not, as the name suggests, an undergarment but an essential part of the dress. The *décolletage* was a deep square with a close-fitting bodice that was open down the centre front and bordered with revers. These were usually double and overlapped slightly (called robings) and came from a band at the nape of the neck that was brought forward to meet at waist level. The opening at the front between the robings was filled with either a stomacher or a sleeveless underbodice. The stomacher was a decorative, V-shaped panel, and was stiffened with pasteboard or busks. The straight, upper border formed the low, square *décolletage*. Decoration consisted of either embroidery or echelles of ribbon. Plain stomachers were usually concealed by large neckerchiefs that encircled the shoulders and bosom, and then fell to the waist where they were tied into position by ribbons. The inverted V-shaped opening at the front of the skirt was pulled back and bunched up to give the effect of a 'false rump' or bustle. This revealed the flounced and embroidered petticoat, which was sometimes partially concealed by an apron. The bodice's sleeves ended just below the elbow in turned-up cuffs. Sleeves were pleated at the shoulder, the join being concealed by the robings. They fitted close to the armhole and then widened towards the elbow. Sleeves were wide enough to allow the full chemise sleeve and ruffle to come through.

Later, the wide-flowing dress, known as the sack gown, came into fashion. This (in silhouette) was a large shapeless gown, not unlike a bell tent; it was simple, very wide, and open down the front, with characteristic long, wide pleats or folds hanging from the neck down the back. Innovations to this gown include double or triple pleats that were stitched down from the neck to the shoulder and then allowed to fall free to the hem. At the front, triple pleats were sewn down the shoulder seam or held by a loop and button to allow fullness on either side of the front edges, which came to a point at the

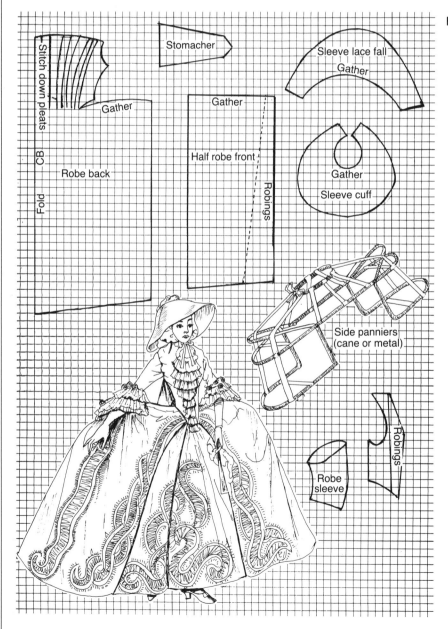

Figure 2.26 The pannier hoop

Figure 2.27 Men's clothing of the eighteenth century

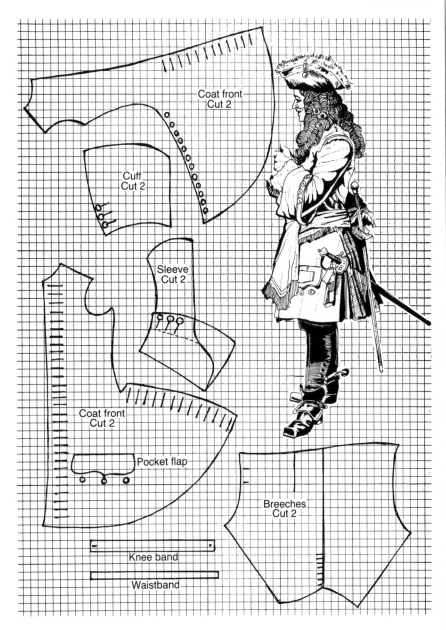

waist leaving a space that was covered by a stomacher. The sack gown was usually secured by loops and buttons. Underneath, the gown was secured by ribbon ties or it was sewn up—if the latter, it was put on over the head. The skirt's fullness was sometimes caught up into the side placket holes.

When panniers came into fashion, these were worn under these dresses. With the introduction of hoops, the petticoat was first reinforced with cane hoops, which soon de-

veloped into various forms of contraption: from pannier style to funnel, dome, pyramid, and elbow pannier styles. Short, padded petticoats lined with horsehair came into fashion.

The hoop fashion has to be studied carefully as there were so many varieties. Hoops could be of cane, whalebone, wire, or osier rods held in position by ribbons. The first structure resembled the shape of baskets worn either side of the body, and this was known by the French word, *panier* (see Figure 2.26). This did not

Figure 2.28 French fashions: *Incroyables* and *Merveilleuses*

extend all the way round but was an oval bell that extended sideways, with a circumference of 11 or even 18 ft (3.5 or 5.5 m). The bell hoop was dome-shaped and varied in size. The smallest was called a pocket hoop. Hoops were worn throughout almost the entire period.

The closed robe (later known as the round gown) was a close-fitting bodice and petticoat that were joined together, frequently with an opening at the front of the skirt. The wrapping gown was a variation of the closed robe. This had a round *décolletage* and a close-fitting bodice with no robings. It had a wrap-over front continuous with the skirt that could be wrapped either to the left or right or loosely. If loose, it was secured with a brooch or ribbon girdle. The low *décolletage* was filled with a lace tucker and modesty piece. The loose-fitting sleeves were three-quarter length with turned-back cuffs, from which emerged double or treble ruffles. The wrapping gown was worn with almost any hoop of the period.

A second style of closed robe was the edge-to-edge closure of the bodice gown. This bodice was similar to the wrapping bodice: it was close fitting without robings and had a low, round, *décolletage*. The front had an edge-to-edge closure formed by jewelled clasps or hooks-and-eyes. The back of the bodice was close fitting and joined the skirt in the *corsage en fourreau* style. The skirt was made with a front fall that, when pleated into a waistband with strings, was secured at the back under the bodice. Gathered together, these pleats hid the pocket slits. The sleeves had narrow cuffs. A modesty piece and a tucker were always worn. A third variation, the sack, was worn as a closed robe until the middle of the century, when it became an open robe. Fashionable colours were blue, cherry, cinnamon, green, pink, purple, red, rose, scarlet, and yellow.

The outdoor wrap was the mantle—a tent-like garment to accommodate hooped dresses. This was ground length, had a hood, and a large, turned-down collar. It fastened with buttons down the front from neck to hem. It was also sleeveless and had two large placket slits on either side. Cloaks (when worn) were usually thigh length and hoodless.

The term 'handkerchief' was given to a lady's neckwear. This was usually a large square of gauze, muslin, linen, lawn, or silk, and it was folded diagonally and placed round the neck. The long ends were secured at the front with ribbon ties. They were often striped or had coloured spots. Black was used only for mourning. The modesty piece was a piece of lace attached to the top border of the corset at the front and placed across the lower part of the *décolletage*. It was not continued around the sides. The tucker was a frilled edging for the low *décolletage* robe bodice, carried up round the edges. Ribbon neckbands fitted closely round the neck, high under the chin, and hung down from the neck and over the bosom, usually in a ruched ribbon. A ribbon girdle was secured at the front with a knot, or jewelled buckles, which were also popular.

Aprons were considered an elegant and decorative part of a woman's dress. For fashionable ladies, the apron was without a bib but, for ordinary wear, bibs were worn. Aprons could be long or short, and were tied round the waist with running strings threaded through the top hem. Often they were made of a fine, transparent material, such as muslin, and were decorated with a floral or spotted design. Shorter aprons were usually wider and knee length, made of coloured silks, brocades, or satin. Colours ranged from blue, black, green, pink, red, and white to yellow.

Men's clothing changed very little during this century, and what changes there were were mainly whims in the detail of cut. Differences between dress and undress were reflected in the type of material used: for undress or everyday

Figure 2.29 Eighteenth-century American clothing

wear, duffle, camber cloth, damask, cut velvet, or satin were used; for formal, full dress and for the court, gold and silver fabrics, brocades, heavily embroidered cloth, and flowered velvets were used.

For neckwear, the earlier falling collar was replaced by the neckcloth, which was basically a strip of material about 1 ft (30 cm) wide and 2 ft (60 cm) long. This was placed round the neck and knotted at the front. Variations were created in the manner of its tying. The cravat (a strip of lawn, linen, or muslin) was worn round the neck and tied loosely under the chin. A steenkerk was a lace cravat that was very loosely tied at the front, and its ends passed through a buttonhole or were pinned to one side. The stock was a piece of linen pleated into a high neckband with a stiffener and secured by a buckle at the back. The solitaire was a black, broad ribbon tied to the running strings of a bag wig, and its ends were arranged in various ways. Workmen wore a pleated handkerchief knotted at the front.

The French Revolution was a turning point in the history of fashion, as Paris was the arbiter of the fashionable world. In women's clothing, the general silhouette became elongated with the abandonment of hoops, petticoats, corsets, bustles, and protrusions. White, transparent, high-waisted dresses of muslin, without undergarments, became more widespread as women's clothing aimed for greater simplicity.

Les merveilleuses (the trendsetters) were represented by the *robe en chemise*. This basic dress was a flimsy, transparent, muslin chemise. Its bodice was gathered at the neck and under the bosom and joined in one with the skirt, which gave an extremely short waistline. *Décolletage* varied. At this time it was worn very low, revealing more of the bosom than concealing it. The waist was encircled by a slim, ribbon girdle. The skirt was ground length and fairly close fitting. Excess material from the hem was draped up and carried over the arm, thus revealing a great deal of leg. All gowns were high waisted and had long skirts. Two styles eventually emerged: the gown-and-petticoat type and the gown-over-gown type, both in the open-robe style. In the gown-and-petticoat style, the bodice was short with a wrap-over, usually with a low *décolletage* and a roll, 'Capuchin' collar. The bodice was secured at the waist with ties or buttons, which were hidden by a ribbon girdle. The bodice was also cut to allow for deeply inserted armholes, which gave it a very narrow appearance. The trained overskirt was open from the high wrap-over in an inverted V-shape. This opening revealed the petticoat, ground length and untrained. Sleeves were either three-quarter length with a slight half-sleeve or were wrist length.

In the gown-over-gown style, the bodice had a low *décolletage* tied or laced at the front with the undergown revealed above it. The overskirt was little more than a broad tail-piece; it was trained and was in a contrasting colour to the underskirt. The sleeves were either long (to the wrist) or half-sleeves, which revealed the long sleeves of the underdress.

The chemise gown was high waisted and of muslin, cambric, or calico. It was ground length and was sometimes so transparent it was necessary to wear tights underneath it. A modification to this dress was a lower neckline and the waist closer to the bosom. Short sleeves were worn; otherwise they were non-existent. The train was longer than before.

With hoops discarded, the greatcoat became fashionable. This was three-quarter length and it was worn with a girdle. The spencer (a short-waisted coat without skirts) was close fitting and had a roll collar and sleeves to the wrist. This coat was very popular with muslin dresses. Shawls made their appearance. They were made of cotton and silk.

Men's coats remained close fitting and they did not have flaring skirts. A curving away from the waistline was very predominant, and coats were fastened with buttons and button-holes from neck to waist. The military coat, with its narrow, turned-back lapels from neck to waist, was adopted for civilian wear. Sleeves were long to the wrist, where short cuffs emerged. By the end of the century, a sham cuff was worn.

Waistcoats were now a pair of foreparts with a back lining and they were sleeveless. Under-waistcoats came into fashion, appearing above the turned-back lapel of the over-waistcoat. Breeches became closer fitting, and the knee-band fastened just below the knee. Pantaloons were close fitting, following the contours of the leg and finishing above the ankle.

The frock-coat was worn for all undress occasions. Its collar, at first, was flat and then, later in the century, high standing. The curve away from the waistline in the skirts became narrower. It was single breasted with no lapels; later it was worn double breasted with lapels. From the earlier loose-fitting sleeves, close-fitting sleeves with vertical slits became more popular. The greatcoat was very large and loose, reaching to just below the knee. Its neck had a double (or treble) falling, broad collar, fastened in a single-breasted fashion to just below the waist. The man's spencer was a short jacket with a stand–fall collar.

THE NINETEENTH CENTURY

(See Figures 2.30–33.) The engravings and caricatures of the nineteenth century are worth studying as they emphasize the extreme high fashion that was so prevalent and popular at this time. Women's clothes underwent great modifications. In the earlier years, all dresses were untrained and their hemlines were pro-fusely adorned with multiple flounces and frills. The trimmings used were floral designs of artificial flowers, silk leaves, vandyked borders, and piped materials decorated with beads. The elegant 'Grecian bend' was achieved by insert-ing elongated rolls securely under the skirt's waistline. Bodices were high necked for day wear and, for the evening, low necked and wide in style. Dresses did not have folds and were close fitting to reveal the contours of the body. This style is not the same as the diaphanous flimsy dress worn between 1800 and 1805. Day dresses were worn with a taffeta pelisse (mantle) that had a standing collar and raised shoulder epaulettes. Round the neck was a neck ruff of pleated lace in two or three layers. The waistline was becoming more natural. The redingote (a development of the Greek-style wrap-over tunic) had a broad, turned-over collar with long, full, puffed, and gathered sleeves.

The spencer remained in fashion—a short jacket with long sleeves that was worn over a dress. A slight modification to both the spencer and the bodice of the dress was the short, puff shoulder sleeve that was worn over a fairly loose sleeve and gathered at the wrist. Although short sleeves were worn at this time, long sleeves were more popular and fashionable and, therefore, they appeared in more styles. Often, longer sleeves were tubular or in the small leg-o'-mutton style.

A study of the court dresses of the time is made easier by the fine examples to be found in museums. English court dress was a mixture of styles. The hoop and pannier were worn with the newer, high-waisted fashion, and this produced a most unbalanced silhouette that had lost the charm and beauty of the old. The French court had long since discarded hoop and pannier contraptions. By 1820 the English had adopted the style of the French: the long, elegant, close-fitting dress with its long train.

Riding habits were a great part of the female fashion world. These followed the men's style and, hence, military-style decorations prevailed. The masculine neckcloth, which was high to the throat, could be seen over the bodice. The bodice was frogged across the front. Over this was worn a tailless, close-fitting jacket, which was frogged and braided and had a high-standing military collar and epaulettes. The skirt was high-waisted, gored, and it fell with side frogging. Skirts varied in colour, some being bright greens and purples. Wraps and shawls remained popular throughout the period, with such added features as long scarf-capes, lace fichu (small, triangular shawls), and pelisses with and without capes.

The real transition, however, was in men's clothes. Men followed the caprices of the 'dandy', and their 'patrons' were the Prince Regent and Beau Brummell. The new style was

Figure 2.30 Early nineteenth-century American costume

typified by its smartness in cut and fit and its attention to the smallest details. However, the colouring of the coat and buckskin breeches (or tight, ankle-buttoned pantaloons) remained sombre. As previously, the frock-coat remained in fashion in both single- and double-breasted styles. The frock-coat was originally a full-skirted garment of military origin but, by the nineteenth century, it had become the most fashionable aspect of men's clothing, the double-breasted style proving most popular.

The frock-coat's waistline was now cut low, and the cut-away tails curved back over the hips and hung either a little above the back of the knee or were long to well below the knee. Its collar stood high at the back and low at the front; its lapel usually had an M-notch or remained plain. Pockets were either secreted in the pleats or were flapped, usually at waist level. Sleeves were close fitting on the arm but were gathered at the shoulder and were generally padded. At the wrist they had a slit and two or three buttons; the stitched-down cuff came well over the hand. The dandy fashion

brought with it the use of corsets and padding, the latter often being added to the chest to give a pigeon-breasted look. The fashionable colour for coats was a lightish blue and they were adorned with brass buttons, although coats were of more sombre colours, such as black or brown. Waistcoats were worn both single and double breasted, with either a broad or a narrow collar. The high, broad collar was usually supported by thin, whalebone ribs sewn in the front edges. A waistcoat's hem was usually cut straight across but the pointed style was also popular. Pockets were not always present but, if they were, they were usually horizontal slits at waist level. The fabrics used were embroidered buff kerseymere and patterned and striped marcella. For evening wear, a white piqué fabric was worn.

Cloaks went out of fashion and the single-breasted greatcoat became more popular. This was fastened with three or four straps or buttons down the front. It was calf length and the back had buttoned pleats. The greatcoat had no lapels but a high-standing collar.

Another style of coat was the Garrick, a garment with numerous capes in multiple layers—also known as the box coat. The male spencer was an extraordinary fashion. This was a short, waist-length coat without tails that was popular for a while with men and then became more fashionable with women.

Neckwear continued to be the stock (neckband)—either black or white for the day, made of muslin, printed cottons, chintz, silk, or gingham but for the evening of silks, satins, gauze or organdie.

For women, the ruff was now replaced by a flat shoulder cape with a narrow frill at the top. However, the chemisette, tucker, and ruff remained in fashion. Long stoles were also worn, with wide, flat collars that covered the shoulders and the bosom; the fichu-pelerine had tails that fell down the front and tucked into a belt, sometimes hanging to the knee. Silk cloaks and mantles in various forms were popular in shoulder or waist lengths. Older women preferred colourful shawls, tippets, and fur tippets.

Male fashion centred on London continued

Figure 2.31 The pelisse dress, about 1825

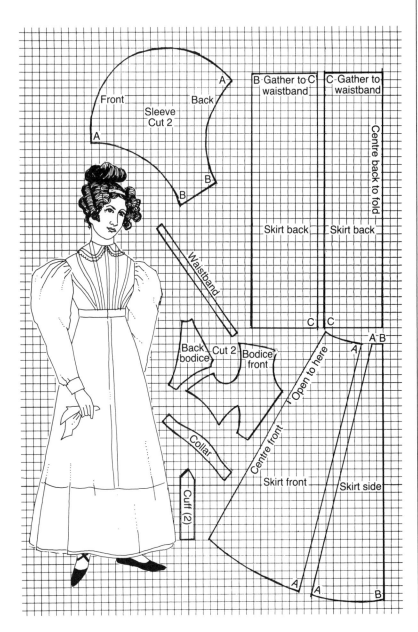

to be—in undress style—the frock-coat, which now assumed its basic shape (with only minor modifications) for the rest of the century. It was close fitting, flared out, and fell in folds to knee level (later it became shorter, to just below hip level). The rolling collar had a V- or M-notch with lapels that ran almost to waist level. The sleeves ceased to be full at the shoulders and became long and close fitting. Waistcoats were now longer in the waist and had a slight dip at the front; they had rolled collars and lapels that reached just below mid-chest. In the more extreme fashions, waistcoats were in harsh, bright colours with broad purple, crimson, and salmon stripes. Breeches were worn on ceremonial occasions; pantaloons (secured under the foot by a strap, or with side slits when worn with such half boots as Hessians) became more popular. Pantaloon trousers were less full than previously and fitted close to the ankle. The costume designer of this period has no excuse for not using colour: the sombreness of the later part of the nineteenth century was not yet in evidence. Fashionable dandies wore light-tan

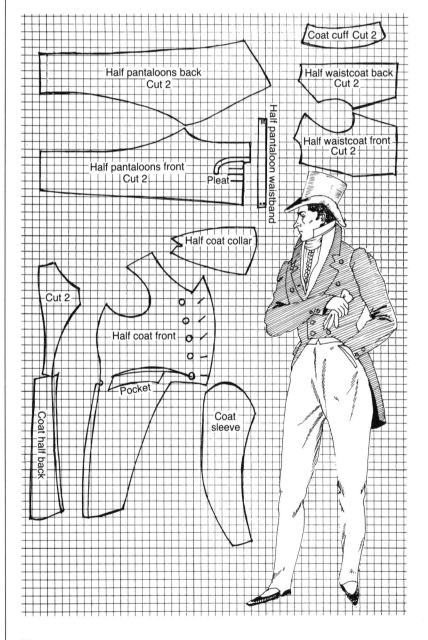

Figure 2.32 The Beau Brummell English style

Figure 2.33 The frock-coat, late nineteenth century

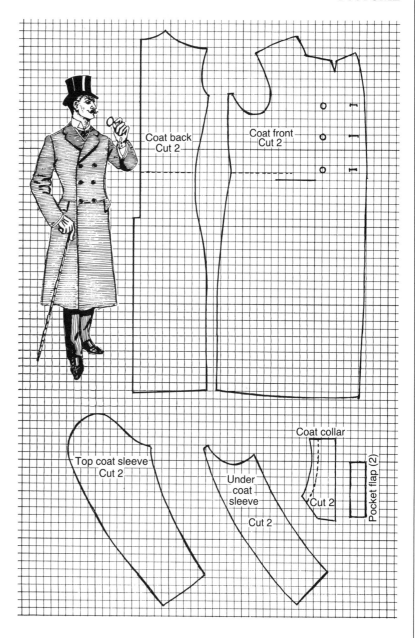

coats, sky-blue satin and violet satin waistcoats, off-white nankeen pantaloons, and yellow stockings with violet clocks (patterning). Plain shirts were taking over from the frilled front style. Outdoor garments, however, remained virtually unchanged. Sporting attire for riding, shooting, and hunting was also very fashionable. Because photography was making its first appearance at this time—through the theatrical scene painter, Louis Jacques Mande Daguerre (1789–1851)—the designer's job of research is greatly helped.

The chief characteristic of the women's clothing silhouette in the mid-nineteenth century was a large circumference at the base of the dress. Horsehair petticoats with further padded petticoats and stiffly starched underskirts all contributed to this effect, which became progressively wider with the introduction of hooped cages—in other words, the reintroduction of the crinoline. The bodice was longer in style and pointed, and V-shaped pleating and a wide, low *décolletage* both came into fashion. The bodice was now stiffened with bone supports that spread up in a fan shape from the waist. The jacket bodice and the gilet-corsage (shaped like a man's waistcoat) styles were close fitting and fastened down from the neck to the waist. The former style ended in short basquine, often worn with a separate skirt. The bodice opened down the centre to the waist to reveal a lace or muslin chemisette.

The front-fastening jacket gained in popularity. This was close fitting to the waist and had short basquines as well as a bodice and also long basques that came over the hips. Sleeves were much shorter and were often wide, to reveal frilled undersleeves. Skirts became wider. The full skirt was gathered at the waist by organ pleating, which consisted of a tubular type of pleat. This, along with the horsehair petticoats and the padding, produced a domed silhouette. Flounces were the popular skirt ornamentation; these made the skirt flare out at the hem from the corseted waist. To decrease the number of petticoats needed, a cage-shaped or hooped skirt (the crinoline), made from fine steel hoops, was created. This device extended the wide skirt to a circumference of 12–15 ft (3.5–4.5 m), and was adopted by all classes. The vogue was for broad collars with large sleeves, as earlier. Cloaks and mantles followed various fashionable styles. Close-fitting jackets with tight sleeves were also popular; these were finely embroidered in the manner of the eighteenth century.

For men, while the frock-coat still dominated the fashion scene, the M-notch was losing favour to the V-notch. The riding coat was now often worn as a walking coat. The single-breasted, hip-length jacket with a small collar and lapels was also popular. Waistcoats were now shorter. Trousers were closer fitting with under-the-foot straps. Still popular were trousers with tops pleated to the waist that were wide at the hips and tapering towards the ankle. Large bows, often with pointed ends and worn over a cravat, were common.

By the 1860s, the fullness of women's dresses had disappeared, and skirts were gored to fit the figure at the waist, although they were still wide at the hem. The crinoline was losing popularity to an eighteenth-century fashion revival—a long, plain skirt with a flounced hem over which was worn a pointed bodice. The material at the back of this skirt was bunched up over a new metal contraption, the bustle. Hence, the silhouette was now a flat-fronted skirt with a curved back and full, protruding posterior. Most dresses now had double skirts with large bouffant shapes at the back, and the upper skirt was caught up at its sides to form an apron effect at the front. Three-quarter length cloaks continued to be fashionable in various styles and with various sleeve modifications.

Men's fashion was now also more relaxed. Frock-coats were no longer waisted, and their skirts hung down fully. The lounge jacket and morning coat were now more fashionable, as was the double-breasted reefer jacket. Waistcoats were cut straight across the bottom and were now short waisted, and were always worn with single-breasted jackets. Trousers were close fitting and were made with fly fronts. Knickerbockers (based on the early style of breeches) were popular for country and sportwear. High neckwear was replaced with stiffened collars, of which there were now many varieties. Popular outdoor garments were the Chesterfield, the Inverness, and the Gladstone.

The last two decades of the century were the forerunner of things to come: a struggle of fashions began. The bustle disappeared, as did wires and stuffed contraptions. The double skirt with its draperies lost favour, its place having been taken by the gored skirt that fitted the hips and flared from the knees to the ground. From the 1890s the corset was deeper, covering the bosom and hips. False bosoms were worn to give a full-bosomed effect. The narrow corset that slimmed the waist to the 'wasp' waist produced the hour-glass silhouette. Tailored outergarments (following the men's fashion of the Chesterfield) were either ground length or three-quarter length.

Men's clothing, on the other hand, followed earlier styles with certain slight modifications. Trousers varied only in width, being now narrow at the top, tight at the knee, and wider at the ankle. By 1896 peg tops had become the fashion: wide knees and narrow, turned-up bottoms. Ironing a crease down the front of each trouser leg became (and remains) the fashion. Neckwear increased in size, becoming 2–3 in (5–7.5 cm) high and appearing in many variations. Outdoor garments were the Chesterfield, the Ulster, and the Raglan coat.

THE EARLY TWENTIETH CENTURY

The characteristic feature of the woman's silhouette at the beginning of the twentieth century was the S-shape: a large bosom, small waist, and large posterior (Figure 2.34). The bodice blouse was high necked with turned-down collars and long puffed sleeves (reminiscent of the leg-o'-mutton style). The ground-length skirt was straight and slightly flared. A special corset was designed to be worn with the S-shape silhouette, which remained popular throughout the Edwardian era. Dresses were now generally in two parts: the bodice and the skirt. The bodice (called a blouse) was usually high necked and pleated down the front. Blouses were often pouched and worn below the waistline at the front. Blouses were generally white but sometimes the same colour as the skirt. They were decorated with pleats, ribbons, tucks, with inserts of lace and embroidery, and with false revers. Jabots (lace frills) and bolero fronts were in vogue. Blouse collars could be square at the front and round at the back. Sailor-type collars were very much in vogue. Diaphanous blouses were fashionable but were always worn with a chemisette underneath. Blouses were usually worn tucked inside the skirt. The long sleeves, which were usually close fitting and ended with cuffs, could be turned back.

Skirts were gored or pleated to emphasize the smallness of the waist, and they were belted to enhance this slimness further. They were to ground length. When walking, the skirt was lifted to reveal the ruffled petticoats underneath. Hobble skirts made their appearance in the first decade of the century. These were narrow towards the hem and often a bias band was added to the base. A braid fetter, which kept the skirt in at the leg, was also sometimes attached.

Costumes (two-piece suits) were popular, and these were worn with a blouse or shirt. Jackets were either single or double breasted, and their fronts were either square or pointed. Collars and revers varied. Occasionally they were large but roll collars and lapels were also popular. Sleeves were often puffed at the shoulder, being pleated into the armhole. Jackets were hip length or even as low as the knee, and were fastened with large, decorative buttons. These two-piece suits were fashionable, as were tailored coats and skirts for country, sports, travel, and town wear.

Motoring outfits were waterproofed; fur-lined top coats were long and voluminous enough to wrap around the legs. A soft, Shetland-wool veil was worn for winter motoring. There were summer-motoring dust coats and light, gauze veils with enormous hats that were tied down with the veil. Goggles were an essential part of the equipment and were worn with both winter and summer outfits.

Belle époque fashion owed more to a lady's corset-maker than to her dressmaker, for it was only through the wasp waist and the arched back of the corset design that her figure was achieved. From about 1910, day dresses were normally one piece. The bodice's drapery gradually became less elaborate and skirts became plainer. High collars remained fashionable but the V-shaped neckline became popular, along with the Peter Pan or standing collar. Pannier effects on skirts were achieved by bunching the tunic just below the hips.

At this time also, dresses with Magyar sleeves were becoming popular. Skirts generally became straight and tubular, and were decorated at the hem with ribbons or down the sides with decorative buttons. When close fitting they were slit up the sides, sometimes with insets to give more width. Later came the wrap-over skirt.

By about 1910 evening dresses were also generally made in one with bodice and skirt.

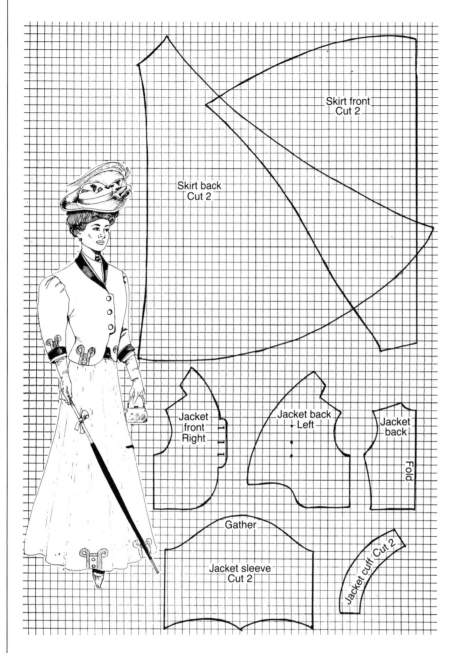

Figure 2.34 An early twentieth-century fashion

Skirt front
Cut 2

Skirt back
Cut 2

Jacket
front
Right

Jacket back
Left

Jacket
back

Fold

Gather

Jacket sleeve
Cut 2

Jacket cuff Cut 2

Tunics and overdresses were still worn, the latter often being draped or in two parts, front and back. Loose tunics had large armholes that were sometimes open to hip level, and which were secured with lacing or ribbon bows. Evening blouses were similar to those worn during the day, but were more ornate and often with embroidered embellishments. The low *décolletage* drapery could be crossed over the front and the back. Fill-ins were often flesh coloured. Gowns with high waists became fashionable, the bodice part merely resembling a sash held up by shoulder straps. For dancing, a fuller skirt was worn, which could be sunray pleated or gored, and which ended just above the instep.

Bathing costumes of the 1900s were a basqued tunic and knickerbockers. They were either made in one or separate with a knee-length skirt. At first they were always in red or navy-blue serge with a white braid decoration. Other colours began to be accepted, and the ornamentation (apart from the braiding) was either embroidery, bows, or decorative buttons. For golfing and shooting, long skirts were worn but jackets followed the men's fashion of the Norfolk jacket. Blouses or shirts had high, stiff collars. Tennis clothes were usually white linen dresses or skirts and blouses: the skirt reached to just over the instep and the dress was usually in the 'princess' style, with a straight skirt, a high neck, and a three-quarter-length sleeved bodice. A white skirt and white blouse with a turned-down collar from a V-necked front could also be worn. A straw boater or a ribbon in the hair completed the effect.

Twentieth-century men's clothing began with the frock-coat becoming unfashionable as the American lounge suit became acceptable as everyday wear. This was cut more loosely than the previous coat. Trousers, although still narrow, had turn-ups and creases. Colours varied but were mainly grey, navy, and brown. The fabrics used were striped, plain, or herringbone tweeds or worsted. The Norfolk jacket and breeches were still popular throughout this period for sports and country wear. For formal dress, the black, broadcloth, cut-away coat with a grey waistcoat and straight, grey-striped trousers without turn-ups were worn. Outer garments (such as the short overcoat) went out of fashion; plain or tweed-patterned coats came in. These were loose, single breasted, and reached to mid-calf with large hip-pockets.

Figure 2.35 Male Russian costume

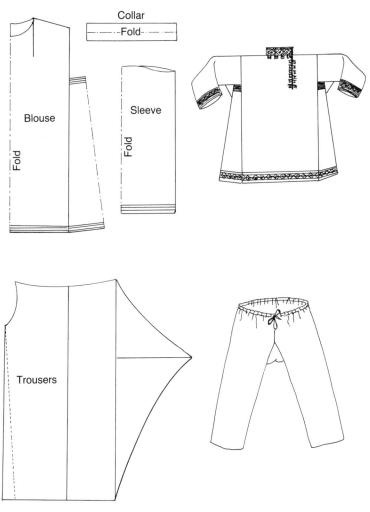

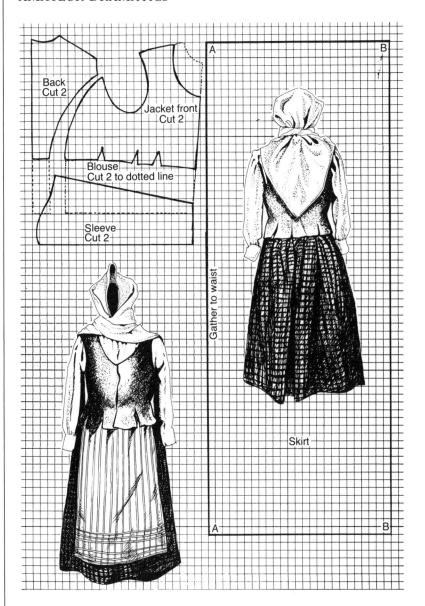

Figure 2.36 Female Russian costume

Velvet and felt collars were the vogue. All coats had raglan or inset sleeves. Soft, white shirts with stiff collars and cuffs were usual, although coloured, striped shirts with a collar to match were often worn. The high collar was popular until World War I, when the lower style returned.

The war years of 1914–18 brought changes. Skirts became shorter, and were flared or fluted and bell shaped. Jumpers became extremely popular and these replaced shirts and blouses. They had no fastenings and were just pulled over the head. They were also fairly long—to the hips. Knitted or crocheted jumper frocks that also just slipped over the head became popular as well. By 1920 skirts had become shorter and evening dresses were now either plain or embroidered brocade, satin, silk, tulle, lace, or georgette. Wide belts and sashes, which could be allowed to trail to the ground, were popular.

Later styles for both men and women are readily accessible to the costume designer. Illustrations are also given for early American clothing (Figures 2.29 and 2.30) and Figures 2.35 and 2.36 show patterns for early Russian costumes.

HEADWEAR

It is more important to get the basic shape of headwear correct than to be accurate in its detail. The aim of headwear, like costume, is to imitate the main characteristics of width, height, and shape and the more obvious accessories, such as veils or hair nets. (For Egyptian headwear, see Figure 2.37.)

Greek and Roman

In Greece, the large petasos or sun hat was worn by men; women wore a variety of nets, veils, and kerchiefs (Figure 2.38).

For the Romans, veils were fashionable for women. Men were usually bareheaded.

Anglo-Saxon to Norman

Viking and Anglo-Saxon men were bareheaded or wore helmets with horns or wings. Women wore a headband or kerchief.

Norman men wore coif-type bonnets or the pointed Phrygian cap. Women wore a kerchief or wimple.

Medieval

Broad-brimmed straw hats and the chaperon (with a liripipe tail-piece) were worn in the early part of this period. Later, men wore coifs, with or without straw or felt brimmed hats with high crowns.

Women wore goffered veils that formed an arch over the forehead. This was made of several layers of material. Alternatively, the head was given the square look, being encased by vertical, metal, ornamental tubes.

Renaissance

Renaissance hats were of great variety, for example, low-crowned hats with their brims turned up or down and worn either square on the head or tilted to one side. The coif was

Figure 2.37 Egyptian headwear

A 'Khepresh' battle headdress worn by Pharoahs

B Nemes (headcloths)

C Close-fitting cap worn by soldiers

D Striped nemes and ceremonial beard

E The Nefertiti headdress

The white crown of Upper Egypt

F The red crown of Lower Egypt

G Duplex wig

H The Queen's vulture headdress

I The double crown

Figure 2.38 Female Greek headwear

usually of white linen and was a simple bonnet that covered the crown of the head. This was often worn by peasants. A velvet cap with ear-flaps similar to the coif was typical of scholars and elderly gentlemen. A tall, brimless, sugar-loaf- or flowerpot-shaped hat was also worn. Wide-brimmed straw or felt hats were still worn by peasants, along with hooded capes. The chaperon style was now worn off the head and was more for ornament than for practical use.

The variety of hats for women was also great. The turban style, with the hair pulled through the crown to hang down the back of the neck, was fashionable, as was the hennin—a stiff, cone-shaped hat that extended to a point and was tied on with a strip of velvet. This was turned back to frame the face. A length of thin gauze floated from its tip. This hat was made of brocade and velvet, and it was worn square on or tilted backwards. Another version, the truncated hennin, had the same

structure but was cut short, giving it a flat end, not a point. The butterfly veil (which radiated out in three wired wings) was also worn (Figures 2.39 and 2.21).

The sixteenth century

During the Elizabethan period, women's hats followed the same style as men's. The Mary Stuart hood was made of lawn or linen and was trimmed with lace. This hat had a dip which formed a curve over the centre of the forehead. Bonnets, such as the taffeta pipkin and the lettice cap, were worn. Hats for riding were of beaver or felt. Scarves and mufflers were made of silk and were tasselled in gold or silver.

Men's hats were worn both in and out of doors (Figure 2.40). These hats came in various shapes, such as the flat hat—a small, round, beret type that had a narrow brim and was decorated with feathers. After the 1570s, crowns became higher, producing the high-crowned bowler. All hats were made of leather, beaver, velvet, or felt and were trimmed with ribbon hat-bands. They were decorated with gold, silver, or pearl buttons and feathers. Decorative undercaps were also worn.

The seventeenth century

Hats were still worn indoors, even at meal times. The Cavalier's hat was made of felt or beaver and had a wide brim and low crown. The sugarloaf style had a tall, conical crown and brims of varying depth that were either flat or curled up. Hats were trimmed with decorative ribbon, silk, or buttoned hat-bands (see Figure 2.42).

The eighteenth century

In the eighteenth century, women wore the fontange—a white lace cap with pleats built up on a wire frame. The pinner was a flat, circular linen cap edged with either a single or double frill. This also had two lappets or streamers that hung down the back or were turned up and pinned to the crown of the cap. Lappets were sometimes tied under the chin, in which case they were called kissing strings. The coif or round-eared cap was bonnet shaped and framed the face level with the ears. Its front had a single or double frill, and it was pulled in by a drawstring to expose the hair. The mob-cap was popular throughout the century. This had a puffed-out crown that stood high towards the back of the head. A deep border framed the face and short lappets hung down at either side. Mob-caps could be worn without further head covering but they were usually worn with a hat or hood. Hoods were popular, and they were either separate items of clothing or were attached to a cloak, and they were made in various styles. Straw or silk hats were also worn that had low crowns and narrow brims trimmed with ribbon or low crowns and wide, floppy brims. The bergere (a large straw hat)

Figure 2.39 Female headwear of the fifteenth and sixteenth centuries

Sixteenth century

Sixteenth century

Fifteenth century

Fifteenth century

Sixteenth century

Sixteenth century

was fashionable throughout the century. This was tied to the head by ribbons that passed from the crown over or under the brim and were then tied under the chin or behind the hair at the back (Figure 2.41). For horse-riding, a three-cornered hat similar to the man's was worn, as was the jockey cap (Figure 2.40).

Because of the universal wearing of wigs, men's headwear played a small part in fashion. The three-cornered hat was the most popular. This had a deep crown that was flat or rounded, and wide brims that were cocked and turned up on three sides. It was worn with the point at the front. The 'round' hat was worn by clerics and workers. This hat's brim was rigid for the 'professional' man and slouched for the 'working' man (Figure 2.42).

The dormeuse was popular among women almost until the turn of the century. This was a large, crowned, caul-type cap that fitted loosely over the head. It had lace side-flaps that were turned back at the temples to expose the front of the hair and forehead. It was trimmed with ribbon bows. The cap shape in general consisted of a large, puffed-up crown with a frill and a trailing streamer that hung down at the back. The calash was a large folding hood with a short cape that covered the large, fashionable hairstyles of the day.

For men, the three-cornered hat remained in vogue. The Macaroni was a smaller version of this, which was placed on the top of a high wig.

During the Regency period, hats for women increased in height and were often covered in the same fabric as the dress. The indoor cap (or cornette) was closer fitting than the dormeuse, and it was secured under the chin with ribbons. Military shapes (such as the classical helmet) were popular. The Quaker poke bonnet, with its nodding feathers, was also fashionable. Leghorn straw hats trimmed with ribbon were also worn, and their ribbons were usually left fashionably untied. A further style was an indoor cap fastened under the chin that was worn with a large, crowned, straw hat with a brim of varying widths. This was turned off the face on one side and decorated with ostrich plumes.

The nineteenth century

The early part of the nineteenth century saw the disappearance of the three-cornered hat as the round hat became more popular. The top hat made its appearance as fashionable headwear. This was made in various forms, the most popular being a hat that widened slightly towards the top.

By mid-century the style of ladies' hats began to overtake bonnets (a hat, unlike a bonnet, was fitted with a crown) in popularity. Hats were worn with their brims up and with one or two ribbons dangling down to the waist. Hat fabrics were crêpe, satin, straw, or velvet. There was a fashion for an excessive ornamentation of bows, flowers, and ribbons under the hat's brim. Large, flat, berets and turbans loaded with feathers became fashionable.

Throughout the century, the top hat remained in fashion for men. Black, fawn, or white beaver and felt was used to make them. Low-crowned hats with extra-large brims were usually worn by country folk.

Early Victorian headwear for ladies was the small cap worn at the back of the head. These often had lappets; others had flowing ribbons hanging down from behind. Early bonnets had wide brims that tied under the chin, framing the face. Bonnets reduced in size by the middle of the century, and had frills round the back and sides. These frills (bavolets) were often large and stiffened with buckram. Nearly all bonnets were tied under the chin by ribbons.

Plain straw hats had, for a long time, been worn by country women. Now the large straw hat (called a round hat) became fashionable for town women. This had a large, flat, mushroom shape and a low crown. It was decorated with flowers and ribbons. A smaller version came into vogue that had an additional narrow lace curtain round the brim. Veils were now also becoming very fashionable.

While the top hat remained the most popular men's headwear, the low-crowned 'wide-awake' hat appeared in various forms and was made of felt and straw. The bowler also made its appearance. Both fur and peaked caps were commonly worn.

Figure 2.40 Male headwear and hairstyles of the sixteenth century

Figure 2.41 Female headwear of the eighteenth century

Large-brimmed hat, about 1789

Loose turban style, about 1785

Large hat with ribbon decoration, about 1796

Low-crown hat with wide brim, about 1799

Although bonnets were still worn in the latter part of the century, a new, higher shape came into fashion. This was the spoon bonnet. Because of the growing height of the bonnet, the inner space was filled with lace and flowers. A bavolet was also added at the back. A study of early fashion plates and journals clearly shows that hats were now more popular than bonnets.

For men (apart from the top hat) soft or hard felt hats were frequently worn—high bowlers and low bowlers—as well as high and low straw hats.

Late Victorian styles were almost the same as previously, but there was an additional vogue for larger hats with pleated brims.

Late Victorian men's styles continued to be the silk top hat, the bowler, and the soft, felt, 'wide-awake' hat. Coming into fashion was the stiff, felt Homburg that had a groove from front to back. Trilbies and straw hats were also fashionable. Caps (the headwear of the working classes) were taken up by the wealthier classes—but only in the country. The masculine Homburg was worn by ladies, both for dress wear and sports activities (Figures 2.43 and 2.44).

Figures 2.45–50 show shoe styles from various periods, and the use of felt in costume and helmet making.

PATTERNS AND MEASUREMENTS

The patterns illustrated are drawn to scale. No allowance has been made for seams and, because of the smallness of the scale, all measurements should be checked against the individual for whom the costume is intended. The patterns have been designed for average measurements, the man's being a 38 in (96 cm) chest, a 30 in (75 cm) waist, and a height of about 5 ft 10 in (1.8 m); the woman's is a 36 in (91 cm) bust, a 26 in (66 cm) waist, and a height of about 5 ft 6 in (1.6 m).

One method of enlarging the patterns (apart from scaling up from the squared paper) is to extend the lines from a given point in as many directions as possible in order to retain the original shape, and hence taking in the performer's measurement to the shoulder, neckline, and underarm. It is advisable to create a measurement sheet for each performer to be

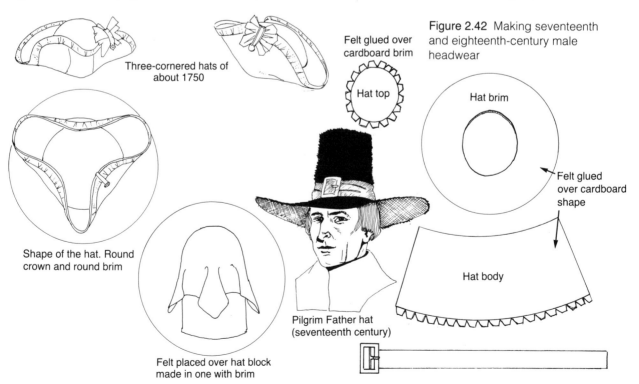

Three-cornered hats of about 1750

Shape of the hat. Round crown and round brim

Felt placed over hat block made in one with brim

Pilgrim Father hat (seventeenth century)

Felt glued over cardboard brim

Hat top

Figure 2.42 Making seventeenth and eighteenth-century male headwear

Hat brim

Felt glued over cardboard shape

Hat body

82

Figure 2.43 Nineteenth-century male headwear

The bowler, 1900

Topper fashion, about 1836

Fashion of about 1815

Top hat and double-breasted frock coat, about 1828

Evening cloak and top hat, about 1820

Figure 2.44 Nineteenth-century female headwear

Hairstyle adorned with small bonnet and flowers, about 1820

Bonnet with ribbons, bows and ties, 1831

Ribbons and feathers, about 1832

Silk hat with bird ornament, 1887

Coiffure with ribbon headgear, about 1825

High-crown silk bonnet, eighteenth century

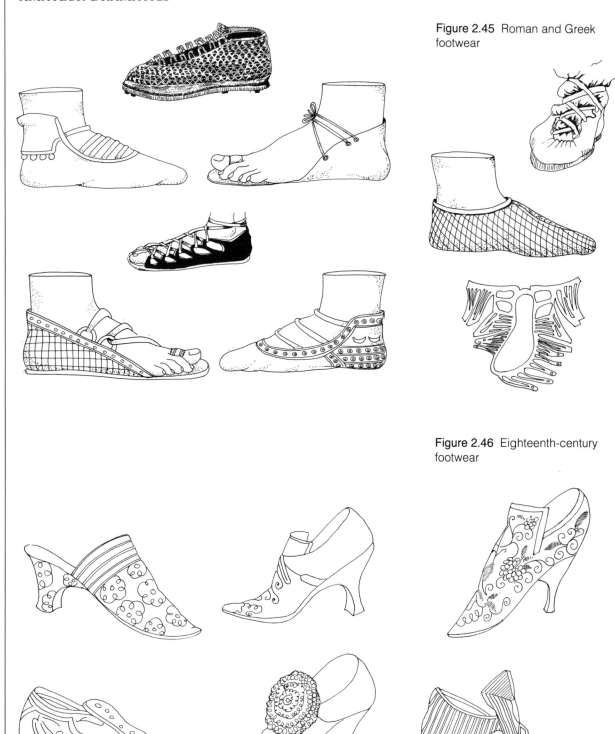

Figure 2.45 Roman and Greek footwear

Figure 2.46 Eighteenth-century footwear

Figure 2.47 Nineteenth-century footwear

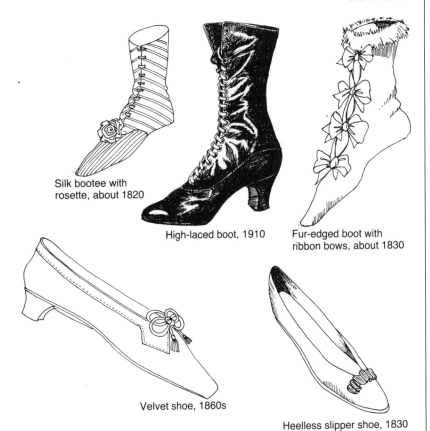

Silk bootee with rosette, about 1820

High-laced boot, 1910

Fur-edged boot with ribbon bows, about 1830

Man's walking high boot of soft leather, about 1814

Velvet shoe, 1860s

Heelless slipper shoe, 1830

Figure 2.48 Twentieth-century footwear

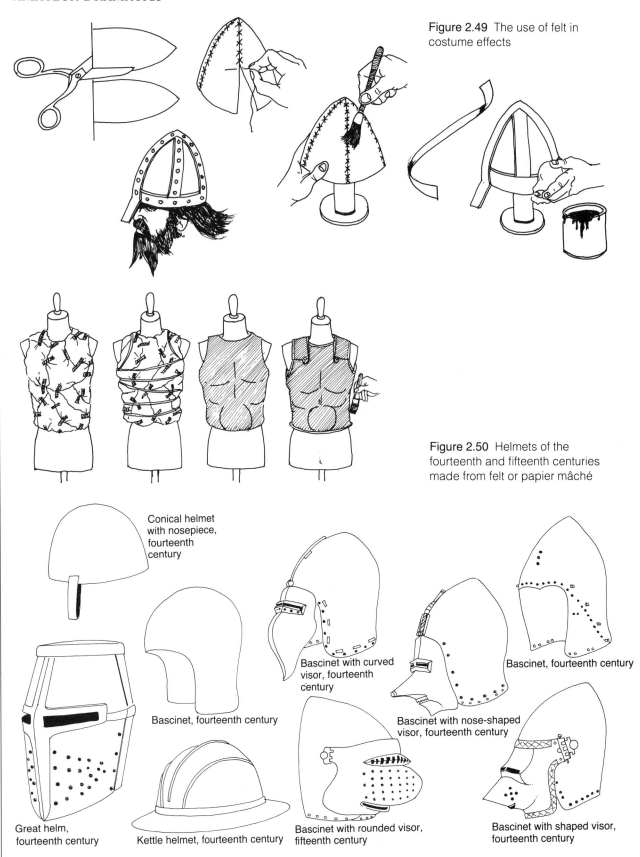

Figure 2.49 The use of felt in costume effects

Figure 2.50 Helmets of the fourteenth and fifteenth centuries made from felt or papier mâché

Conical helmet with nosepiece, fourteenth century

Bascinet with curved visor, fourteenth century

Bascinet, fourteenth century

Bascinet, fourteenth century

Bascinet with nose-shaped visor, fourteenth century

Great helm, fourteenth century

Kettle helmet, fourteenth century

Bascinet with rounded visor, fifteenth century

Bascinet with shaped visor, fourteenth century

dressed, with the performer's name as well as the part to be played noted, as follows:

- Performer's name:
- Name of part:
- Height:
- Chest or bust:
- Waist to hip:
- Waist:
- Hips:
- Length of arm (outside with arm bent):
- Length of arm (inside with arm straight):
- Wrist:
- Width across shoulders (front):
- Width across shoulders (back):
- Shoulder to floor:
- Waist to floor:
- Waist to knee:
- Crotch to knee:
- Waist to thigh above knee:
- Waist to below knee:
- Width around calf:
- Width around thigh:
- Measurement around head:

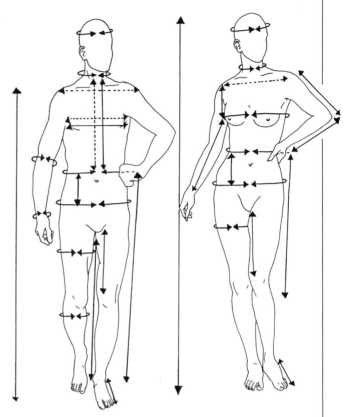

Figure 2.51 Measurement chart

(A measurement chart is given in Figure 2.51.) Measurements should not be taken too tightly nor over any bulky clothing.

For chest or bust measurements, place the tape-measure across the largest part of the body and make sure the tape is not too low at the back. To find the natural waistline, tie a piece of string or ribbon around the waist fairly tightly so that it does not slip. The hip measurement has also to be taken at the widest point, and it is also better to measure how far this is beneath the waistline. For tight sleeves, measurements of the top of the arm at the armpit and around the elbow when the arm is bent are needed. Across the shoulders gives width; this is best taken about halfway down from the armhole at the back. A garment's length is measured from the nape of the neck to the natural waistline. The nape at the back is slightly higher than the shoulders.

The patterns are basic designs that can be built up or altered to suit the costume designer's ideas. Many modern patterns can also be adapted, especially for skirts and trousers.

Modern tights can be used extensively to build on, and two separate pairs (in contrasting colours) can be halved and rejoined to give a parti-coloured effect.

3

Make-up and wigs

INTRODUCTION

With the exception of acting there is no other facet of theatre that is so clearly an art as make-up. Make-up cannot be taught; it is a craft acquired through trial and error, practice, and careful study. There is no end to learning it: make-up is in a constant state of change as new ideas and new products are introduced. Latex and rubber, for example, have recently added a three-dimensional aspect to the art.

Every play also presents its own make-up problems: the period, the costumes to be worn, and the type or style of hairdressing, whether wigs or the performers' own hair. It is also important to know what expressions and muscular movements the characters will make and then apply make-up to suit each part. Every character will demand a different technique.

Make-up is not new. The Egyptians and Babylonians used make-up for decoration. They wore wigs, applied rouge, pencilled their eyebrows in, and used various powders and lotions. Their hair was powdered with different colours, blue, green, and gold being the most popular. They wore fantastic headdresses and often wore face and head masks. The mouthpiece of Greek theatrical masks amplified the actor's voice like a megaphone. These masks were designed with exaggerated features and expressions.

Today, theatrical make-up (an extension of the mask) is used instead, the main reason being to help the performer take on the physical characteristics of the role. Make-up also projects natural facial features and makes them more distinctive in the high intensity of stage lighting. It can also change and disguise the performer's appearance.

MAKE-UP

While stage make-up consists of various techniques, painting the effects of highlights and shadows is, of course, the most important. Successful make-up is akin to costume: it should, for example, create a convincing transformation of a healthy young person to a dissipated, ageing person within a play's span. A performer's appearance is as important as the costume he or she wears, yet the basic equipment needed is very little.

In the dressing room, a good working surface and a chair are needed. The working surface must be large enough for all the required make-up to be laid out. A mirror with tungsten lighting (never neon or fluorescent) should be large enough so that all that needs to be seen is seen. A wash basin is also very useful.

Applying make-up is really an art in itself, and it requires a certain amount of study and thought. The performer's face should be carefully scrutinized in the light of how the character is to be interpreted. Stage lighting and the distance from the spectators must also be taken into consideration. The performer's jaw line, cheek bones, forehead, and nose should all be studied. As the bone structure is static, facial animation comes through muscle movements. The two most important features of the face are the eyes and mouth, so great attention must be given to these. Apart from the face's structure, skin texture must be noted to determine the type of make-up required. If the performer perspires freely, grease paint is recommended as this leaves no sweat trail-marks.

The basic make-up kit should include towels, a cape to cover the clothes, cotton wool for cleaning up, a hairband to keep the hair from the face, and a make-up box fitted with loose trays, usually of a cantilever type.

The foundation is the basic make-up item itself, and its colour is determined by the character. On top of this the other colours are blended. Two types of make-up base are available: grease paint in stick form (usually applied with the fingers) or pan (water-soluble make-up in liquid form that is applied with a make-up brush or a moist sponge). The traditional form of make-up is grease paint. Grease paint blends with the skin to give it greater tonal graduations of colour than pan. With skilful use and practice, many of the pitfalls in its application will be avoided. For body make-up, water-soluble paint is recommended, especially where it comes into contact with clothing, for example, around the collar and under the chin. Grease paint is very difficult to remove.

Lining colours are narrow sticks of make-up used to emphasize shadows, wrinkles, and highlights, and for lips and eyes. Waxed pencils are available and these are used to accentuate eyebrows, eye outlines, and to touch up lips and wrinkles.

Brush widths are usually no. 8 (0.4 cm) for lips; no. 10 (0.7 cm) for shadows or folds; and eye shadow no. 14 (0.9 cm) for shadows and highlights. A sponge will be needed if water-soluble make-up is to be applied. Squirrel-hair brushes are used for removing surplus powder, which is always applied with a puff and laid on the face to fix the make-up. A translucent type of powder should be used to avoid spoiling the make-up's colour. All theatrical make-up suppliers stock cleansing and removing creams.

Crêpe hair is used by most amateur groups. This is fixed to the face with mastic or spirit gum and removed with solvent. Crêpe hair is made from wool and comes in hanks. These hanks are tightly braided with string that can be unwound, pulled, and combed (Figure 3.1). Hanks will then be found to be some four times longer than when bought. This makes crêpe hair very economical, as it is sold by the metre (or less). It is available in different colours, for example, light brown, dark brown, black, grey, blond, and red. It is, however, desirable to take the crinkle out of the hair by steaming it or damping it in warm water. This must be done sometime before its use so that it can thoroughly dry out.

Performers should learn to work with crêpe hair as, so often, amateur budgets will not stretch to the luxury of hiring beards and moustaches. If a moustache is required, it must be made in two parts for it will be very insecure if made in one piece because of the performer's lip and face movements. Liquid latex (Duo adhesive) is ideal for forming a beard that will be used on several occasions (Figure 3.2). The latex is applied to the face over the area designated for the beard. Crêpe hair, strand by strand, is then placed onto the latex with the

Figure 3.1 Using crêpe hair

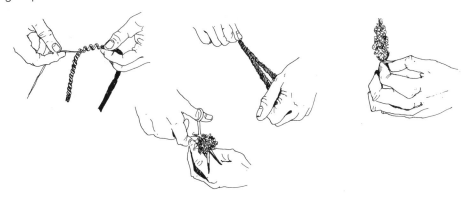

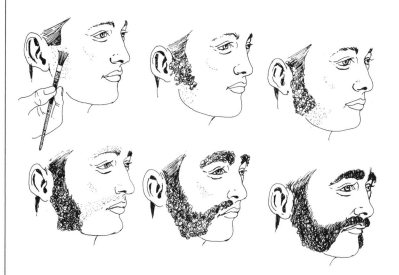

Figure 3.2 Constructing a beard from crêpe hair

fingers until it is at the required thickness (the straight-cut edges of the hair are always laid into the latex). This is then cut to the required length and the process if repeated until the whole area has been covered. Like make-up, this requires practice, both in judging the thickness of the beard and in achieving a realistic mixing of hair-colour tones. Matching hair colour is not easy: under stage lighting crêpe hair has a tendency to appear darker, as it does not reflect light like natural hair. Hence a lighter tone should be used. For example, a dark-haired person will require dark-brown crêpe hair, while a fair-haired one will require the palest of blond crêpe. It is also better to mix hair tones to give a realistic look, using lighter tones on the upper hair and darker ones beneath. Once this has been stuck it can be cut and trimmed as a real beard. Crêpe hair built on latex (after its first use) can be peeled off and used again, being stuck on with spirit gum. Spirit-gum mastic is the adhesive most readily available to amateurs but, if used as a base, this will allow the beard to be used only once. However, if a beard has been well blended it can be taken off in pieces and, with care, used again.

Hair pieces are either of man-made fibre or real hair. These can be hired or bought, and a large variety is available: whole wigs, switches, curls, chignons, toupees, and so on. Beards and moustaches are also available for buying and hiring.

Stage lighting should be the make-up artist's first consideration. Usually, all illumination comes from the lighting battens above the stage, from the wings, and from the front-of-house spots. The strength of this lighting will give an indication of the depth of make-up needed: the brighter the intensity of the lighting, the greater the 'wash out' of colour that will render the performer pale. Coloured stage lighting also influences the type of make-up to be used. The director should be consulted about the lighting plots. Distance must also be closely observed—the audience should, usually, never be aware of make-up, so the closer the audience the less make-up will be required. For example, when working in theatre in the round, make-up should be concentrated on the highlights as shadows show up very strongly. Make-up should always be applied so that the audience at the back of the hall are able to distinguish performers' faces as well as those at the front.

Always use a hairband or net to stop the hair from falling over the face. Remove all clothing that, when worn, will touch the face (if this is not practical, then put the clothing on *before* applying the make-up). Cover the shoulders and lap with a cape or towels to protect them from the grease paint and powder. Clean the face thoroughly, removing all outdoor make-up (if used) with a cleansing cream and then wash the face with water (greasy skin is very difficult to work on). The base colour can be a mix from a wide range of colours, and the best mixing-palette for the beginner is the hand. With practice, however, the colours can be mixed directly on the face.

Applying grease paint is best done with the fingers. First, make up the cheeks as close to the side of the nose as possible. Then apply the make-up to the centre of the forehead and work outwards, covering the face evenly and just sufficiently to hide the complexion. Too much grease paint becomes unmanageable. If a water-soluble make-up is being used, apply this with a damp sponge or make-up brush. Next apply shading and highlighting. The darker colours are applied first, and then the highlights on the areas that catch the light. Always blend outwards, making sure you leave no harsh edges.

Having applied basic make-up, powder should be patted on generously and carefully with a powder-puff. Flesh colour or white can be used according to the effect required. Surplus powder should be removed with a soft brush.

Eyebrows and eye lashes should always be last. Touch in the eyebrows with an eyebrow pencil. To accentuate or alter the eyebrows, they should be flattened with eyebrow plastic or, more simply, by applying moistened soap. The eyebrows should then be covered with the basic make-up, powdered over, and the new shape drawn in. Eyelashes should be cleaned with a wet finger to remove any make-up or powder that may be clinging to them and then, for women only, mascara should be applied with a small brush or wand.

If the director is 'type casting' then make-up need only be used to the minimum. The following sections describe the basic techniques of make-up: straight, ageing, and character.

Straight make-up

Straight make-up is make-up applied in correct depth of colour to allow for the brilliance of theatre lighting and to compensate for the loss of clarity because of the distance of the performer from the spectators. This make-up should not in any way alter the features or character of the performer. The more intense the lighting, and the greater the distance from the spectators, the greater will be the depth of colour to be applied. It is essential, first, to study the skin's natural colour, the intensity of the lighting, and the size of the auditorium.

Men

For men, the foundation required is Leichner No. 5 and No. 9 grease paint. Combined, these give an average, healthy, robust and glowing complexion. The grease paint is applied by broad streaks on the forehead, down the nose, under the eyebrows, down each cheek across the chin, under the nose, and under the chin slightly down the neck. These streaks are blended together in rotary movements (but not too hard) until the face, ears, and behind the ears are smoothed out and the whole face is covered with enough base make-up to hide the performer's natural colouring.

Cover the face carefully: the neck (back and front) and ears are just as important as the basic face. If these are not covered well, the result is a 'mask' when expanses of white skin can be seen in these areas. Never leave 'bare' spots through which the natural skin shows. These look a strange grey against the healthy glow of the foundation. Also, if these are left unattended, when powdered the make-up will look spotty and patchy.

The cheeks must be blended in very carefully, leaving no distinct harsh lines on the base make-up. A series of small dabs of Leichner No. 3 Carmine should be applied on the cheekbone and under the outside corner of the eye. This is then blended in with the finger tips. The mouth should be cleaned of base make-up and just a little No. 9 added. If this is overdone the effect is likely to appear effeminate.

The eyes are the most important feature and they require a great deal of care and attention. The shade of grease paint to be applied will depend very much on the performer's natural hair colour and colour of eyes. A blue-eyed, fair-haired or light-brown haired person will need a grey—possibly No. 31 or 32. Blue paint should never, on any account, be used. For mature roles, browns No. 28a and 28 should be used. For dark-haired males, No. 28 is better, being a dark brown in tone. A few dots should be placed on the upper lip and then blended in with the finger tips, leaving no harsh line. Blending should not extend to the brows but should reach to just a little beyond the extremity of the eyes—this enlarges the eyes slightly.

Cover the make-up with translucent powder from the chin, and work upwards pressing the lambswool pad (this gives the best result) with a firm movement until the grease-paint base is completely covered. Remove surplus powder with a soft 'baby' brush or fluffy puff. Watch out for any shiny patches—apply more powder until these disappear.

Finishing the eyes is now the final and most important task of theatre make-up. Brilliant illumination tends to make the eyes look smaller, and so they must be outlined with a black or brown lining pencil, again depending on the performer's hair colour. Draw a thin line along the bottom eyelid as close as possible to the eyelashes, extending just a little further than the natural corners and curving downwards fractionally. Next, draw in with the eyeliner a thin line along the edge of the upper lid close to the eyelashes, beginning from the inner corner of the eye. Again, continue the line a little beyond the corner of the eye in a slightly upward curve, fading it into the make-up with the finger tip and not allowing it to join the lower eyeline. This makes the eyes appear larger. A small dab of white or flesh-coloured grease paint can be added to the space between the two eyelines. A further red spot can be added to the inner corners of the eyes, and this is sometimes outlined. If the eyebrows are well defined there is no need for any make-up. Simply wipe over to remove the base make-up and powder or, if need be, a light neat line of eye marker may be added. Heavy eye make-up can alter a character's whole personality.

All skin seen by the audience should be made up: arms, legs, or any other part of the body. Grease paint in this case is not very suitable, and a body-coloured liquid or cream is advisable. These body colourings can be easily washed off with warm water and soap.

Women

Straight make-up for women varies little from a man's basic foundation. The base is usually Leichner No. 2 for lighter complexions and No. 2½ for slightly darker skins. There are other colours and these can be tried out. Carmine No. 2 or 3 are very suitable and usual for cheek make-up, lips, and the corner spots for the eyes. Similar to men's cheek make-up, a larger spot of Carmine should be placed on each cheekbone in line with the outer corners of the eye. A few smaller dabs are added under the eyes towards the nose and slightly above the outer edge of the eyes towards the temple. The deepest colour should be in the centre and this should be blended in with the base foundation over the temples and towards the eyes and down the cheeks. Again, no harsh edges should be seen. Then, with the residue still on the finger tips, work the colour under the eyebrows without touching the eyelid itself, and then blend a little spot on to the point of the chin. As for men's make-up, the neck and ears must not be neglected, and liquid or cream must be applied to avoid any trace of a 'mask'. All parts of the body exposed to the audience should, again, be painted.

The amount of eye make-up depends on the period of the play, but normally the following colours can be used: blonde, red, brown, and black hair with blue eyes, shades of blue Leichner No. 325 and 326; red or blonde hair with green eyes, green Leichner No. 334–336 or blue and green mixed (blue No. 39); and blonde, red, brown, or black with brown eyes, No. 28 and 28a. With the correct liner, make a few dabs along the eyelid. Allow the deepest colour to remain at the bottom and blend the rest up the carmine-blended colour under the eyebrows. Shading of any sort under the eyes should be avoided, unless called for in the character's role in the play.

All make-up should now be covered with translucent powder, removing all surplus with a soft brush or fluffy powder-puff. Any tell-tale misses that appear as shiny patches need more powder until they are eradicated. It is important that the puff is perfectly dry; any dampness or too much picked-up grease paint on the puff can ruin make-up. It is good practice to keep pads and puffs clean and, on occasion, to wash them with warm water and soap.

Enhancing and enlarging the eyes is the next step. It is essential that both eyes receive the same treatment, otherwise the make-up will be ruined. With a liner of the appropriate shade, a thin line is drawn along the edge of the lower lid, from the corner to just beyond the eye in a slight, downward, curve that fades away into the temple colour. Next, outline the edge of the upper lid from the inner corner and extending beyond the eye in a slight upward movement but not allowing the line to meet the lower line. In between them, add a touch of white or flesh colour. This lengthens and enlarges the eyes. Clean off any excess powder or base foundation on the eye lashes and apply mascara. Each lash should be treated separately. Work only on the underside, preventing any lumps of grease paint to form at the ends of the lashes. Apart from giving an odd, cross-eyed look, these lumps could fall onto the face and smudge the whole make-up. Unless required or the performer is quite used to them, false eyelashes are not recommended.

Eyebrows follow much the same pattern. These should be cleaned of any base make-up and powder. If they are neat they can be combed into a fine line and shaped with a brown or black eyeliner or eyebrow pencil. They must, however, be extended to follow the line of the enlarged eye, and both must be balanced, one with the other.

The mouth is the last part of the make-up to be applied. First the lips must be cleaned of all base grease paint and powder. With the mouth slightly open, begin at the centre of the upper lip and, according to the shade required (usually a grease-paint stick of Carmine No. 2 or 3), apply in a upward and outward curve over the top of the lip and then down with a round movement towards the corner of the mouth. Finish before reaching the extreme corner—unless the part calls for a large mouth—as this is the effect created if the corner is reached. The lower lip should be painted with a centre dab and then blended both left and right, leaving a space of equal length unpainted towards the corners of the mouth. An additional, painted, fine outline of white can be added above the upper-lip top to define its shape. Lips, however, should not be too heavily made up—rather an 'unmade-up' effect should be strived for.

The black performer's make-up
The black or dark-skinned performer's face make-up differs only slightly from make-up for white or fair-skinned people. Black performers have the advantage that they can use their own natural skin colour as a base, which is not possible with lighter skins. They may, but not always, require a different shadow, blending the mixture in equal parts of reddish-brown, black and a dark brown, which is made heavier or lighter to suit the face. If, however, a build-up of features is required, putty is used and the appropriate base colour must be found to cover it and then blended into the natural skin colour. Highlights can follow those used by the lighter-skinned or a make-up of gold can be laid on the projecting parts and blended in carefully, then applied along the length of the lips. Otherwise, make-up is the same as for the lighter-skinned. Eyes are carefully outlined with a black eyeliner, mascara is used on the eyelashes, and eye make-up is blue or green with perhaps an orangey-brown colour for the lips.

Ageing
Ageing by make-up is only achieved by studying older faces, which vary considerably, and is perhaps best done with the hair and costume as, if not done carefully, make-up can produce a caricature effect. The lines of expression become more fixed or deeper as the muscles droop or sag. The foundation is usually a pale colour as older people's circulation is poorer. The skin has a greyish-ivory colour. Dark-brown paint lines are applied to the forehead, following the contours of the face, and at the temples, the bridge of the nose, the inner corners of the eyes, and the folds beneath. These are also applied down the fold of the

nose and lips, and down the cheekbones. Draw in the drooping corners of the mouth and continue these over the chin. Draw in also the folds in the neck and jaw line. This colour is blended into the base foundation with the finger tips. A white or light-colour highlight is added next to the marked shadows, following the contours of the face. Blend the highlights with the base foundation and the shadows.

Cheek colouring has to be kept low and away from the eyes: this creates the illusion of sagging. The lips should be in a thin curve with a slight downward trend at the corners, and expressive wrinkles should be applied to the forehead and between the eyebrows, with soft shadows representing hollows in the cheeks and temples (use a grey liner, Leichner No. 31). Deeper shadow (Leichner No. 32, grey) should be reserved for the socket space between the eyes and the nose, and these should be applied with little shading lines.

Next, powder the whole make-up. For men, apply a dark-brown pancake make-up over the beard area, the sides of the cheeks, under the nose, and on the chin very lightly, with a fine stippling sponge.

The hair should now be treated with a light, ivory-coloured pancake, starting at the parting until the hair is completely covered. Then apply some hairspray. Use Leichner No. 20, white, to age the eyebrows and eyelashes. The eyes should be lined with Crimson Lake to redden the rims.

Teeth should be painted with nicotine-coloured tooth enamel. Tooth enamels can also be bought in black and white. Tooth make-up can be effective if used in the correct way. The appearance of broken or missing teeth can be achieved by simply painting the teeth. This effect should never be overdone as it can look very unpleasant if too much enamel is applied. Enamel is easily removed with a tooth brush or fingernail.

A woman's base foundation make-up should be a light colour of ivory blended well into the hairline as a wig may well be worn. Apply brown shadow lines, following the contours of the face and neck. Blend into the foundation as

for men's make-up. Highlights are then applied next to the shadow lines, and blended in with the finger tips. Thoroughly powder the face, including the neck. Dipped in red carmine make-up, use the stippling sponge very lightly from the inner eye position, down the nose, and under the cheekbone. The lips should be left unpainted to leave a dry, pale look.

Hands are just as important as the face—elderly hands go with ageing features. Apply the base foundation as for the face, and line in the shadow colours on the backs of the hands and down the sides of the fingers. Add highlights next to the shadow lines and blend in. Nails can be clean or a pencil line can be applied to give a nicotine-stain effect under them. Completed hand make-up should be well powdered.

False features

Nose putty should be approached with caution and not used unless it is absolutely essential. If the occasion does arise, the following must be carried out carefully.

Nose putty is a skin-coloured type of modelling clay that is applied before any make-up is put on the face and after the face has been cleaned of all grease (see Figure 3.3). A few short strands of rolled-up crêpe hair stuck on the nose with spirit-gum mastic will act as a key to hold the putty firmly. Avoid all areas that are mobile: the centre of the forehead, the mouth, and along the jaw. The putty is kneaded until it becomes very malleable and then shaped into the desired form. The edges should be as thin as possible and smoothed down with a make-up remover. The putty is now pressed firmly onto the crêpe hair and the nose smoothed out and blended into the skin. The edges are again smoothed with the make-up remover until the putty and skin are one without any join mark. The base foundation is applied and patted onto the nose putty. A stippling sponge gives a slightly florid effect and this helps to hide any visible hard edges. To remove the putty, take a strand of strong cotton and run it down the nose—similar to cheese-cutting wire.

There is a wide range of special effects in

Figure 3.3 Using putty to create a false nose

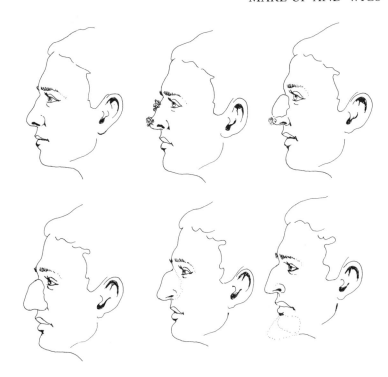

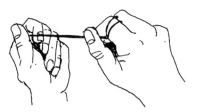

piece of strong thread to remove putty .

make-up but they should be used with care and moderation. If carefully applied and carried out sensibly, these can heighten a character's dramatic effect. With skin-coloured nose putty and derma wax, variously shaped noses and chins can be simulated, as well as scars and wounds. Both materials are self-adhesive, but wax is the more malleable of the two and used for more subtle modelling. With experience, liquid plastics, such as Old Skin Eallodien and Tuplasst, can be painted on to the skin as an alternative. These give a very realistic effect. They dry on contact with the skin and wrinkle as they do so.

Disfigurements

Facial disfigurements are achieved in two ways: with make-up or liquid latex. The 'black-eye' effect is made with a mixture of make-up colours (red or carmine, yellow, green, and blue) mixed together on the hand or on a make-shift palette. This is then patted around the eye. A further few spots of yellowish-green and blue will heighten the effect. A freckled-face effect is best achieved with a light-brown make-up spotted on with a cotton-bud stick in an irregular, light pattern.

Latex is used for localized wounds, sword cuts, and gun shot, etc. These effects can be purchased from theatrical make-up shops but they are, however, quite easy to make. A little latex in a bowl, a sheet of plastic or glass as a palette, some soft tissue-like paper, and a brush (cheap and disposable) are all that are needed. For a raised, swollen effect, brush a small amount of latex onto the palette (Figure 3.4). Allow this to dry and then lay rolled soft paper on top of the dried latex. A further layer of latex is then laid on top to cover the paper. When this is dry, a further thinner coat is applied. When dry, powder generously with talcum powder, remove carefully from the palette, and apply talcum to the back. The area where the face wound is to be is cleaned of all grease, and mastic is applied to the back of the latex and this is stuck to the face. To hide any hard edges, apply a little latex around the edges and leave it to dry. When dry, the base foundation is applied, and this should be carefully patted on. Highlight the raised areas and darken the lower area with a carmine. This method can be used for all facial, arm, and leg wounds.

Larger wounds can be simulated with gelatine. This is made up with equal parts of water, and the gelatine and water are then heated. Glycerin is then added and a few drops of artificial blood. The skin is cleaned of all grease and, while the mixture is still warm, it is applied to the area required. Gently spoon it on. As it dries, use the spoon or fingers to model the disfigurement. The lower parts are made up with dark make-up and the upper parts highlighted. Blur the edges with the stippling sponge dipped in a deep-red make-up.

Special-effects theatrical blood should be used with great care as it can stain and ruin costumes. Recommended is Leichner Casualty Simulation and Kryolan Special Film blood, which are available in two colours, light or dark. Leichner mouth capsules effervesce 'blood' when crushed in the mouth. However, blood sachets can be made quite simply by soaking a sponge in liquid 'blood' and then encasing this in cling film. In a stage fight, the cling film is squeezed and the 'blood' will pour or seep out. Kryolan Fix Blood is a gel that remains glossy when dry. It peels off easily but is rather expensive. 'Blood'-dripping knives, whose handles can be squeezed, can be hired.

Innovations in plastic have considerably altered stage make-up effects. The addition of silicone has given a more natural 'new look' to older make-up methods and made them much easier to apply and remove. Plastic ingredients are used in putty make-up, and new adhesives have been developed, such as water-based spirit gum. Plastic, acrylic, fibre hair is now used in wig-making, producing a more life-like effect.

WIGS AND HAIR

Wigs and make-up go hand in hand, as make-up is the all-embracing name for the disguises it creates and of which wigs are a part. Special latex or rubber caps are available from make-up manufacturers. The object of these caps is to produce a bald-head effect. These caps can be made but they require a great deal of expertise—it is better for amateurs to purchase them. Bald-head caps are made in a strong, thick material that generates a great deal of make-up work and patience to hide the joining line. These thick caps are less expensive than the thiner ones (that have an almost undetectable hair join) but the disadvantage of thinner ones is that, unless great care is taken, they can tear on removal.

Caps are fitted over the head and then stuck to the forehead with spirit gum (Figure 3.5). They are then carefully blended with the face base foundation. Ideally, the best make-up for a cap is pancake applied first with a brush and then an overlay of further pancake which is patted on. To free the cap from the head, release the back, then the sides, and pull the cap forward over the head. The cap is cleaned with soap and water, dried thoroughly, and stored safely in as open a position as possible.

Before embarking on the wearing and hiring of a wig, study the performer's own natural hair. Apart from the expense of hiring, the performer's comfort has to be taken into consideration—a wig may fall off, etc. Also, only the more expensive wigs are undetectable with their invisible, gauzed hairlines. When the

Figure 3.4 A facial disfigurement

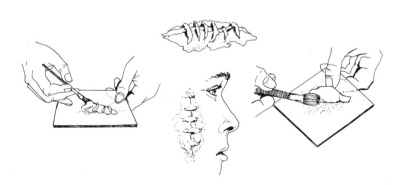

Figure 3.5 The rubber-cap technique

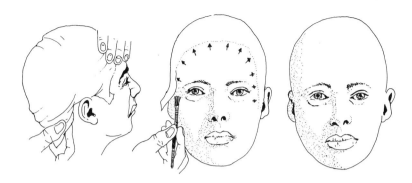

make-up is complete the wig can be fitted. The hair should be combed back as flat as possible and covered with a cap made from the top of a pair of old nylon tights. This is tied with a knot and the stocking cap is pulled on from the front, backwards over the hair. It is lined up with the hairline and fastened to the natural hair with slides on either side of the forehead and at the nape of the neck (the same procedure is applied if a man has to wear a wig). The wig is positioned starting from the front; it is pulled to the back and secured at the nape of the neck. The wig must be pulled back until it fits the head comfortably and almost reaches the natural hairline. Position the wig finally by holding its front and pulling it back as far as possible. It is then secured with large hairpins that are slid through the wig at the front into the hair and under the cap. Pins on either side of the head, at the front, and behind the back of the neck, will ensure the wig stays in place.

Most amateur groups will have access to a hairdresser and, with their help, the careful styling of the performers' hair will create convincing historical accuracy. Small hair-pieces, false plaits, and switches can also be added. With the performer's consent, a little dyeing will add to the realism of the part. Modern products are available for this that will not bother the recipient too much. Most large stores sell cheap, modern wigs that can be adapted for most plays, and the range of hair colouring and texture in these wigs is very convincing.

If, however, the part demands something rather special, and if the budget is large enough, a well-known reputable wig company will be able to supply a wig of the correct style, shape, and size. It is the costume designer's or the wardrobe department's job to give the wig company the correct information: head measurements, colour and style, and preferably a clear drawing of the wig chosen. Arrange fittings for the performer if necessary, as a good fit is essential, especially if the part calls for a great deal of action (Figures 3.8 and 3.9 show how to measure the head). In preparing the drawing for the hire firm, do not lose historical accuracy. The best way is to present both a front and back view of the head with all the relevant information: characterization, colour, and facial hair (sideburns, beard, and moustache), which should be drawn in with a clipping of the performer's own hair for matching.

PERIOD HAIRSTYLES AND MAKE-UP

Research into hairstyles usually starts at libraries and art galleries. Sculpture, in particular, gives a good idea of detail as this is three dimensional.

Egyptian and Biblical

An Egyptian man's hair was usually black and wavy. Slaves wore a round bob that was cut in overlapping layers and that exposed the ears, being cut longer at the back. Wigs were used extensively by both sexes and were made of various materials, including real hair and wool, and they were worn in many lengths and thicknesses. They were also dyed in various shades of blue and red. Wigs were often covered in a painted cloth (Figure 3.6).

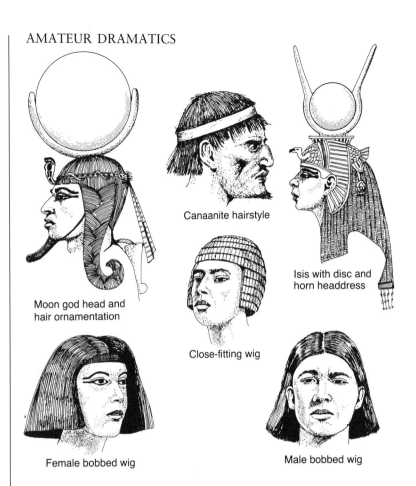

Figure 3.6 Egyptian and Babylonian facial and hair decoration

Moon god head and hair ornamentation

Canaanite hairstyle

Close-fitting wig

Isis with disc and horn headdress

The lappet wig

Female bobbed wig

Male bobbed wig

Egyptians were usually clean shaven, but on ceremonial occasions high dignitaries wore a postiche (a false beard) in the form of a thin cylinder 6 in (15 cm) long that hung from the tip of the chin.

Egyptian women normally wore their hair long over their shoulders, the ends finishing in tight ringlets. Wealthier women wore wigs of coloured hair. Hair was also ornamented with ribbon fillets or a single, cone-shaped piece 4–6 in (10–15 cm) high, which held perfumed ointment. Ornaments were worn on the head to signify rank: the royal uraeus, the lotus, the asp, sacred feather, or the isis. Queens wore the crowns of the Upper and Lower Nile. The hat characteristic of royalty was a stiff, tall hat ornamented with the uraeus and a painted fillet. They used lighter shapes to make themselves fairer than their menfolk. Women's lips were rouged with carmine and their cheeks were painted pink. Fingers and toes were treated with orange henna. Eyes were shaded with a deep blue and then completely outlined with a bold, black line that extended beyond the eye towards the temple. Kohl (charcoal) or ash and lead were used for this.

Babylonian, Assyrian, and Persian men wore long beards that were thick and curly and cut off square at the bottom. Head hair was also black and bushy and was often worn at shoulder length. It was dressed behind the ears and had a straight fringe over the forehead. Symmetrical waves were fashionable. Lower orders wore their hair naturally with a headband. Women's hairstyles were also shoulder length.

Hebrews wore their dark hair in semi-long waves that were glossed with oil. Beards were long and neatly trimmed. Women's hair was heavily plaited, and the elaborate braids hung with gold ornaments. A close-fitting cap, a head scarf, or fine netting was always worn.

Greek and Roman

Greek men at first wore their hair long and gathered at the back in a knot; later this was considered effeminate and so shorter hair became the fashion. Beards, too, became unfashionable, and only older men wore them. These beards were stiff and painted.

Earlier hairstyles for women were ringlets—thin, snake-like curls held in place by fillets. The more fashionable later style was hair neatly tied back with a knot, or a chignon held in place by a fillet or headband. The Greeks were naturally fair but used dyes and wigs.

Roman women sported complex, elaborate hairstyles. The hair was dyed or bleached, and false pieces of blonde or red hair was often used. This was braided and coiled, and frizzed and curled in high build-ups at the front. Men's hair was short and crimped with irons into short curls on the forehead and at the nape of the neck. If beards were worn they were short and close cut. To be clean shaven, however, was the fashion.

Anglo-Saxon to Norman

Viking and Saxon men wore long braided hair. The beard, when worn, was likewise long and braided. Large moustaches were worn without a beard. Women wore their hair long and loose. When married, the hair was braided and drawn up with pins.

Norman hairstyles varied from the long to the short. The head was often shaved at the back level with the ears and the remaining hair cut short and brushed forward. Longer hair was parted in the centre, and had a fringe or was brushed back. Long moustaches and forked beards were worn, but being clean shaven was more popular (Figure 3.7).

Women's hair was parted at the centre and was long. It was interwoven with ribbons and an ornamental casing of metal cylinders. False hair was often used. Monks' heads were shaven in two styles: the Roman tonsure and the Celtic tonsure.

Medieval

In the early medieval period, a bob style of collar-length hair that was waved or curled in a single scroll-curl or ringlets was typical for men. Men were also, in the main, clean shaven.

Figure 3.7 Hairstyles: Anglo-Saxon to Norman

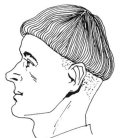

Noble women and young girls wore their hair long and loose. The hair was parted in the centre and tied either in a bun on the nape of the neck or in a chignon down to the shoulders. With the neck bare, the hair was encased in a gold mesh or crispin.

The later medieval style for men continued to be the bob, which was usually curled and worn to jaw length. Beards were becoming popular. They were clipped short or single or double pointed, and were worn with short moustaches. Later, the short pudding-basin style came into fashion.

Later medieval women (if married) wore their hair up and encased in elaborate forms of headdresses. Unmarried women sported long hairstyles that were often crowned with floral decorations. Foreheads were often shaved to give the impression of a high brow. Eyebrows were plucked, and dyeing the hair with saffron was popular.

Renaissance

Men still wore bobbed hair trimmed to moderate lengths and that was straight or curled. Some cuts, however, were bushy at the sides, and the page-boy cut with a fringe was popular. Clipped short beards or moustaches were often worn.

Long hair was normal for unmarried girls. Their hair was braided and hung in centre-parted plaits. When a hennin was worn, the hair was shaved or plucked where it was visible at the sides. Later, when worn further back on the head, the hair was not shaved.

During the Elizabethan period, ornamented dressed wigs, false hair pieces, feathers, and dyed hair were all the vogue for women. Red and blonde colours were popular. Powder and rouge were used, and patches of silk and velvet in various shapes and sizes were applied to the face with a mastic gum.

Elizabethan men cropped their hair all over and then brushed it away from the forehead and stuck it down with gum. Cropped beards and moustaches were also worn. Later, longer styles of hair were fashionable, reaching the shoulders in the love lock: a tress of very long hair that was plaited and had a ribbon tied at the end. This was then brought forward to hang over the chest. Short beards, such as the vandyke, picke-devant, spade beard, square, and marquisette, were worn. Wigs, patches, and make-up were worn only by the dandies of the period. Masks of velvet or silk that covered the whole face were worn to conceal identity.

The seventeenth century

Seventeenth-century men were usually clean shaven, although moustaches and vandyke beards were still worn. Wigs were also worn. The coiffure for ladies was the fringe over the forehead and loose, short, hanging curls on either side of the face and a flat bun at the back of the head. The hair was decorated with ribbon, plumes of feathers, and lace pieces. Paint and powder, and perfume and patches, were fashionable. Masks were still worn.

In the late seventeenth century, various new hairstyles came in for women. Corkscrew curls were massed on the sides above the ears, and the hair was brushed back. A flat bun at the back was popular. Long ringlets that crossed the shoulders or closed, massed curls all over the head were also popular. These styles were decorated with ribbon loops, bows, and top knots. Make-up was used extensively, particularly mouches or black patches. Cork plumpers were placed in the mouth to fill out the cheeks.

For men, hair was worn long to the shoulder. Wigs became fashionable and grew longer as the century progressed. Moustaches and beards became unfashionable, although were still occasionally worn.

The eighteenth century

Eighteenth-century women's hairstyles varied from high, frizzed, built-up curls to the simple hairstyles worn by working women. This simpler style was taken up by the upper classes: curls framed the face while the rest of the hair was fashioned into a knot at the crown of the head. False clusters of ringlet curls were often attached to the back of the head.

For men, the wig supplanted natural hair

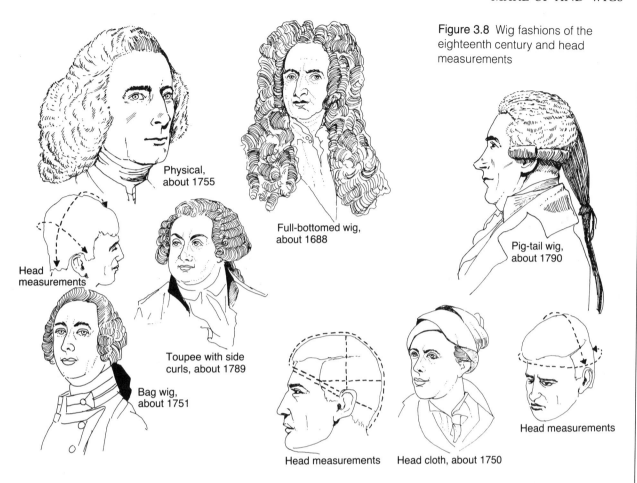

Figure 3.8 Wig fashions of the eighteenth century and head measurements

Physical, about 1755

Head measurements

Full-bottomed wig, about 1688

Pig-tail wig, about 1790

Toupee with side curls, about 1789

Bag wig, about 1751

Head measurements

Head cloth, about 1750

Head measurements

(Figure 3.8). Natural hair was cut very short or even shaven off completely. The strange fashion of powdering the hair with white powder continued throughout the greater part of this century. The dandies and beaux of this period used artificial beauty aids: rouge for the cheeks and lips, patches, padding, padded calves, and perfume and powder.

Hairstyles varied from the very low to the very high. In the 1760s, exaggerated arrangements of towering hairstyles in excess of 1 m were built over pads of horsehair. The basic style was a mass of stiff hair rolls that rose to a peak. This was then plastered with white powder. Much research is needed for this period, and a good hairdresser in the team is essential. Rouge still persisted, but white paint was discarded. Patches were still fashionable. Eyebrows were plucked and false bosoms were worn.

Until the late 1790s, men still wore wigs. (Natural hair became the vogue after this date.) A study of the wigs of this period should be undertaken by the costume designer, whether the wigs are to be made by the team or hired. Dandies still continued with their beauty aids.

The nineteenth century

The early nineteenth century brought for women the high-coiffure, built-up, top-knot hairstyle. Hairstyles became smoother and sleeker, with centre partings and side puffs and curls. For men, wigs were now only worn at court or by legal and church dignitaries. Men's hair was cut short but long enough to be curled, as curls and waves had become fashionable. Side whiskers were worn by men of all classes but moustaches at this time were not fashionable. The hair was often cut short at the back to accommodate the fashion for high

Figure 3.9 Hairstyles of the early twentieth century and head measurements

About 1917

About 1908

About 1910

About 1910

Head measurements

Head measurements

About 1913

Head measurements

Head measurements

About 1909

Figure 3.10 Hairstyles from around the world

Japanese girl with make-up

South American young girl with unusual hairstyle

Creole girl

A Samurai hairstyle

Wig of a Maiko (a trainee Geisha)

Asian old man

collars. Artificial aids were used by dandies: corsets, rouge powder, and dyes.

By the middle of the century, women's hairstyles had changed with the fashion. Popular now was the plait fixed to the back of the head with a large horn or tortoise-shell comb. Fashionable also was the wearing of ringlets at the side of the face. Dyed, red silk 'curls' that hung in two puffs from the forehead and were secured by a band tied round the head were also worn. Younger ladies wore the simple love-lock style behind their ears. Another style was a centre parting with the hair scraped flat across the top of the head and with the sides arranged in falling ringlets. Styles varied so much at this time that the costume designer is given great latitude in choosing. Rouge remained in fashion until about 1837, when a white pallor was thought to be more interesting and romantic.

For men, a centre or side parting with curls was popular. Side whiskers also formed a fringe around the face. The centre-parting style for women prevailed through the early Victorian period. The hair came down from the centre parting in a number of different ways: plaited and then drawn up into a circle to surround the ears, or turned up from the covered ears to be entwined at the back in a knot or bun. Or the hair was allowed to hang in simple ringlets down the back and at either side of the shoulders.

The later part of the century saw the introduction of the chignon, which was often enclosed in a net. This fashion dominated the period. It could be worn low on the nape of the neck, sausage shaped, or rounded with many curls down the back. All styles were adorned with flowers, lace, and ribbons. False hair built over pads was often added.

The late Victorian style of hair was to cut it close to the head, with the fullness at the front and a curly frizz over the forehead. Another late style was the hair dressed back from the forehead, and the back hair pulled up and worn high.

Figure 3.9 shows women's hairstyles for the early twentieth century (and how to measure the head), and Figure 3.10 hairstyles from around the world.

4
Stage props

INTRODUCTION

Stage properties are often considered, wrongly, to be a minor part of stage design. On the contrary, properties often create the atmosphere and authenticity of the set and costumes—all are inseparably bound up with one another. Props are very complex and fascinating and are, perhaps, apart from costume, one of the oldest arts in play acting. So many different materials and skills are needed in the production of props that an active and imaginative mind is needed by the props person. This person is theoretically responsible for everything that is movable on the stage—with the exception of lighting equipment and scenery. Apart from set furnishings, 'props' is responsible for all hand properties, jewellery, and accessories that are worn or carried by the performer as these, especially in an amateur production, are made or supplied by the 'props' department.

The value of a good props team is not so much their adaptability or ability to make props but that they know the stage's correct techniques and limitations, and that they also do not rely on outside contractors. The amateur usually works on a smaller scale and budget than the professional but, nevertheless, amateurs have the satisfaction of knowing that their work is very varied and likely to have a great element of responsibility.

'Props' has to decide how a particular prop or effect should be created, as there are often many different ways of achieving the same result. Props must, of course, work very closely with the stage designer so that both are fully aware of all the factors involved. As props are visual, it would be unfortunate to exclude an effect that may be essential for the play because it appears too complex.

MATERIALS AND METHODS

'Props' has to carry out its work usually armed with the simplest of tools and materials. Yet it must create the most effective illusions in an area that relies so much on trial and error. Many convertible items will be found in the most unexpected quarters: junk yards, second-hand shops, and jumble sales. All kinds of things that are normally thrown away can be used: egg cartons, plastic bottles, packaging, polystyrene, bits and pieces of fabric, metal, pieces of wood, buttons, nuts, bolts, screws, nails, tubing (both metal and cardboard), cork—in fact, anything that can be modified or disguised as something else. Cord and string are also useful as they can be twisted, bound, plaited, and glued to almost anything. Cord can also be used to bind the handles of made-up swords or daggers, or used as edging for mirrors and pictures, etc. It can even be used as hair to make a simple wig. Knotted, plaited, or knitted, string makes very effective chain mail when it is afterwards sprayed with silver metallic colour. Old nylon stockings can be used for a heavy type of chain mail if it is plaited or knotted. Felt is another very useful commodity that can be used in a variety of ways to represent many other fabrics and effects.

The advent of many modern materials, such as glass-fibre compounds, polyester resin, latex, and expanded polystyrene, has improved techniques considerably, and the making of props has become more specialized. Although these new innovations must be borne in mind, it should not be forgotten that older methods are still valid in making props. Clay, sand, wax, papier mâché, and plaster of Paris blended with latex, plastics, and adhesives allow the props department to face their requirements with confidence.

Before proceeding, it must be remembered that stage props are usually large or small articles of furniture in the period of the play. It is essential, therefore, to know the play's atmosphere. Some general observations about furnishings through the ages are, therefore, now described.

PERIOD STAGE FURNISHINGS

Early Egyptian furniture was constructed on simple lines with a wealth of detail (Figure 4.1). It was made of wood, metal, or ivory. The large, throne-type chairs were often carved from wood, then gold plated and inlaid with

Figure 4.1 Egyptian, Greek, and Roman furniture

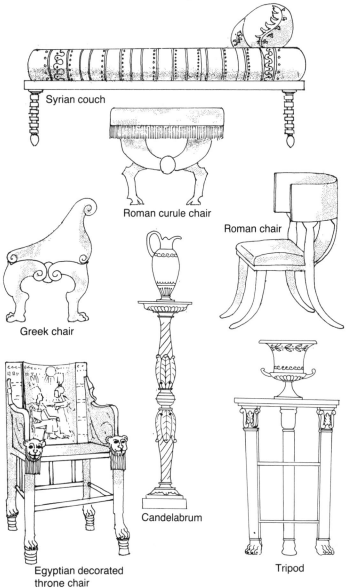

Syrian couch

Roman curule chair

Roman chair

Greek chair

Candelabrum

Egyptian decorated throne chair

Tripod

multi-coloured glass paste, glazed terracotta, and semi-precious stones. Some of the carvings were covered with silver leaf. The armrests were in the form of winged serpents with double crowns. Cane seats were supported by carved animal feet and decorated with animal heads. Chests and coffers were popular, and made of stuccoed and painted wood. Beds and couches were narrow and had painted frames and short, carved, feline legs. Mattresses were often plaited straw. Beds were made with a single endboard at the foot.

Greek furniture (Figure 4.1) followed very closely the style and fashion of the Egyptians but it was made of bronze or wood. Tripods, often of marble, were popular for both religious and domestic purposes. Thrones and foot stools often had legs made of elephant tusks, and stools without arms and backs had carved legs in an animal design. Tables were low and not unlike modern coffee tables. Candelabra and lamps were supported on a base or suspended on a chain. Beds and couches were made with both head and footboards, with mattresses and cushions covered with skins or draperies.

Roman furnishings (Figure 4.1) followed the Greek style but had a little more luxury and sumptuousness.

Early Romanesque, Anglo-Saxon, and Norman furnishings (Figure 4.2) were made of wood, oak, ash, and elm. Furniture at these times was scanty and crude. Beds, often with wooden boards, had rough mattresses and covers of skin and fabrics. Curtains were drawn across them at night. All furniture was strictly utilitarian, being either fixed to the wall or placed against them to leave the main part of the room free of obstacles. Chests were often made of hollowed-out tree trunks encircled by iron bands with large iron locks. These were an essential item of furniture.

Early medieval furniture was still rough and scanty. However, skills did improve with the Gothic style of decoration. Everything was made to be used as a storage place and a seat: chairs were rare, and benches and stools were still used.

Elizabethan and Jacobean furniture (Figure 4.3) was heavy and made of oak. England was late to follow the Italian Renaissance style of

Figure 4.2 Early Romanesque, Anglo-Saxon, and Norman furniture

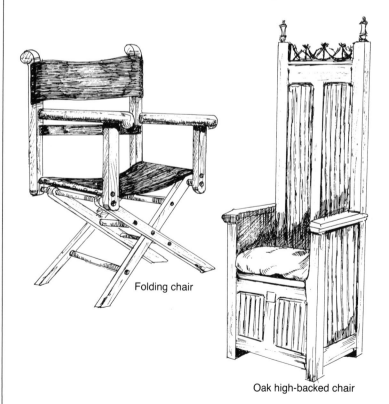

Folding chair

Oak high-backed chair

Oak bench

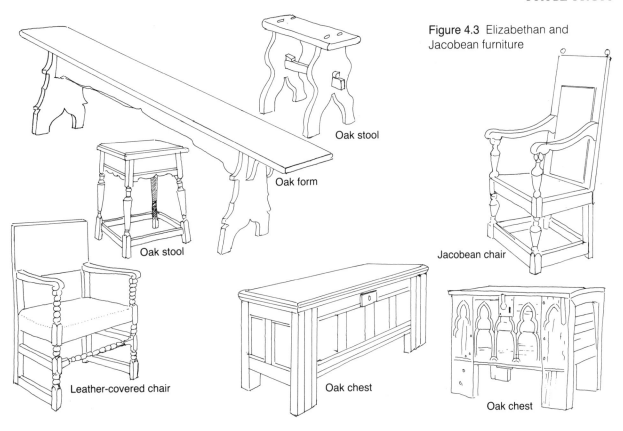

Figure 4.3 Elizabethan and Jacobean furniture

Oak stool

Oak form

Oak stool

Jacobean chair

Leather-covered chair

Oak chest

Oak chest

furnishings, and thus it is permissible to include the old, heavy, Gothic style of furniture in early Elizabethan plays. Later in the sixteenth century, furniture acquired the over-ornate Renaissance style, which was massive and profusely decorated. The chest developed from the plain, crude, wooden Gothic object to an ornate, framed, and panelled, almost elegant, piece of furniture. Chairs were straight, rigidly backed, and upholstered in fabrics of stamped leather, velvets, and brocades secured with braid. With the advent of the farthingale, a special chair was designed without arms, a low back, and a narrow seat. It was upholstered, and the padded back tilted away from the upright. Stools and benches were still in vogue. Tables were large and heavy until later in the century, when they were replaced with smaller gate-legged styles. The most important, costly, and magnificent piece of furniture was the bed. This was usually a four-poster and was heavy and large with a low frame on small posts. This

frame was joined to a heavy, carved bed that had two posts at the head and two posts at the foot. Overall the bed could be almost 3 m high in order to support the returns of the corniced testers. The corners of the uprights on the bed were supported by solid carved columns. To these was attached heavy, richly embroidered tapestry, velvet, or silk that was fringed or edged according to the wealth of the owner.

Restoration plays should be furnished in the new decorative manner of the time—the 'age of walnut' in furniture. Walnut had now replaced oak as the wood used for the new type of carving that had emerged. Upholstery was now commonly used on chairs, settees, and stools. Furniture became more elegant, delicate, and subtle in form compared to the earlier, heavy, oak furniture.

The furniture of the early Georgian period was still in the Baroque style, with carvings of lions' heads, masks, and shells on walnut. When portraying larger, wealthier houses, stage

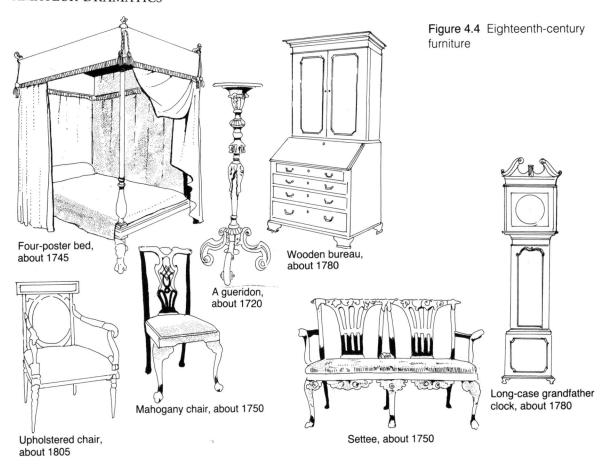

Figure 4.4 Eighteenth-century furniture

Four-poster bed, about 1745

A gueridon, about 1720

Wooden bureau, about 1780

Long-case grandfather clock, about 1780

Upholstered chair, about 1805

Mahogany chair, about 1750

Settee, about 1750

furniture for this period must appear to be rather large and ostentatious. When a middle-class house is to be portrayed, the furniture is smaller.

From about 1730s mahogany furniture became popular because of its suitability for fine carving (Figure 4.4). Chinese and other oriental lacquered furniture in various colours (black, red, yellow, and green) became very popular, especially for boudoirs. A mixing of styles—Gothic, Rococo, and Chinese—continued throughout the period. Small tables were used for the popular tea-drinking habits, and wide-armed chairs were specially designed for the hooped dress. Upholstery was in satin or tapestry. Most local museums have some of this furniture on show.

From about 1770 painted furniture was in vogue. This was painted in floral and festoon patterns. Gilt was used in conjunction with the painted furniture, and this was popular for mirrors and picture frames. Regency furniture followed closely the styles of classical antiquity, with designs from Egyptian (winged sphinxes), Greek, and Roman sources. Such features as brass and bronze gilt ornaments were used prolifically as corner and foot pieces, the latter in a paw or claw style. At this time furniture was graceful and well designed, and a mixture of styles was very prevalent.

The early Victorian period continued to make use of Regency styles until around the middle of the nineteenth century when, with the appearance of great industrial wealth, the demand for more items of furniture became the fashion (Figure 4.5). This was met by mass production, and handmade items became rare. Gothic heaviness returned. The whole atmosphere was one of over-crowding, of accessories (such as stuffed birds, wax fruit, china figures, vases, glass ornaments, mirrors, and anti-macassars), and of tables covered with lace.

Chairs had embroidered covers in wool or silk. A large quantity of iron was used in furniture construction: in bedsteads, garden furniture, and table legs. The elegant line of the Grecian sofa was now replaced by the heavily carved and over-ornamented spiky horsehair settee (Figure 4.6). Throughout this period and into the twentieth century changes were numerous and diverse but all are easy to research.

Domestic and religious utensils are important for authenticity, and good examples are again to be found in local museums. The Egyptians often made pottery with tall shoulders, small handles, and painted bases, often of bronze and alabaster. Some vases were like bowls with handles; others had very long necks with rings of floral decoration inlaid with coloured paste. Oil lamps were made of clay and bronze. Funerary jars with canopies of animal or human-head carvings were made of alabaster, granite, or marble. Baskets of assorted shapes were used for carrying bread, fruit, fish, and other foods. These were made of wicker, reeds, or palm fibre. Highly polished hand mirrors were made of bronze or copper, and their handles were often inlaid with semi-precious stones. Musical instruments were the harp, crotalum, and sistrum.

Greek pottery (Figure 4.7) had graceful lines and pictorial designs so numerous and so well illustrated in books that they hardly need to be explained here. Drinking horns with carved handles and with animal heads at their base were very popular. The lyre and the double flute were the most popular Greek musical instruments. There were also the cithara, syrinx (pan pipes), and the harp. The Romans imitated Greek fashion in nearly all things.

The Romanesque period brought a lowering of artistic standards but brought in utensils of glass, iron, and bronze. Harps and playing horns were the most common musical instruments.

Medieval pottery was often decorated or buff earthenware with a thin glaze. This was used for pitchers, bowls, and cooking vessels. Later, metal cauldrons and skillets replaced pottery cooking vessels. Wood and metal were used for making cauldrons, bowls, jugs, ewers, and buckets.

By the fourteenth century, glass, silverware, and a higher standard of pottery had evolved.

Figure 4.5 Nineteenth-century chairs and stools

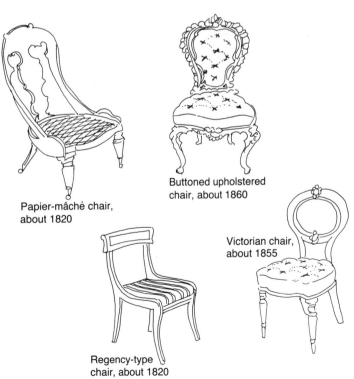

Papier-mâché chair, about 1820

Buttoned upholstered chair, about 1860

Victorian chair, about 1855

Regency-type chair, about 1820

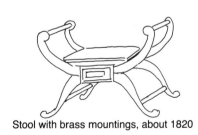

Stool with brass mountings, about 1820

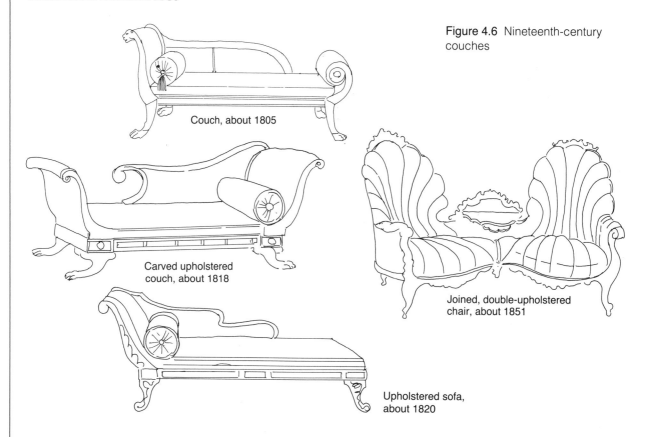

Figure 4.6 Nineteenth-century couches

Couch, about 1805

Carved upholstered couch, about 1818

Joined, double-upholstered chair, about 1851

Upholstered sofa, about 1820

In Tudor times, pewterware was being used by servants and silverware by the masters and mistresses. Spoons and knives existed but there were no forks.

The seventeenth century saw the introduction of reddish or yellowish-brown pottery. Glass and pewter continued in fashion, and forks were imported to England for the first time. During the Restoration, Chinese porcelain became popular, as well as the earlier pewter and silverware.

Georgian utensils were made of wood, brass, iron, earthernware, and glass. Musical instruments were mainly the spinet, vidium, cello, flute, and harpsichord.

The nineteenth century witnessed an upsurge in the use of porcelain, stoneware, and Wedgwood, the designs being based on Greek modes. Glassware, too, became more popular. The harpischord and the piano came into the home. The violin, cello, viol, double bass, harp, guitar lyre, flute, and trumpet were all also in use. Early Victorian utensils were the same as earlier but with the addition of bone china. The pianoforte became an important piece of furniture. In the late Victorian and Edwardian era, Art Nouveau became popular, with influences from Greek, Roman, Japanese, and Indian styles. By 1911 the telephone was in use on a national scale and the portable gramophone became popular in homes.

Many of the items mentioned above are often impossible to hire so they have to be made. Most objects can be cast. The main purpose of casting is to reproduce something in a more permanent and durable material than, for example, its original pottery or glass form, or to make a number of replicas.

MODELLING

Papier mâché

Papier mâché is still an ideal solution to many problems, as it is light, durable, and strong enough to hold its own structure. It can be

Figure 4.7 Greek vases

Greek vase

Fictile vase

Amphorae

Drinking horn

Vase

Fictile vase

Paieras

Lamp

made in various ways (see Figure 4.8). Torn strips of laminated paper and pieces of cloth can be used in one project in alternate layers, or just pulped paper soaked in glue size. To make basic papier mâché, cold water paste as used for paper hanging is needed. (A more economical way is to make one's own paste with flour and water. Half a litre of water is used for each heaped teaspoon of flour. The flour is mixed to a smooth paste with a *little* of the water. The remaining water is boiled and slowly added to the flour paste, stirring all the time to make sure no large lumps form.) The paper has to be torn into strips, not cut—cutting leaves a hard edge. The paper strips are soaked in water, squeezed out, and the paste is applied.

When using papier mâché, it is advisable to use two types of paper: an economical newsprint and a plain, coarse, sugar-paper type so that each layer will be different. When enough layers have been applied, finish off with a thin tissue paper to give a smooth surface. When the object has been allowed to dry completely, a

layer of shellac paint will give a good seal. For large objects such as tree stumps, use a cotton material cut on the cross to allow for give. Dip the material into a pot of glue size or carpenters' glue and lay it on in layers. An armature of wood and chicken wire is the framework for this type of prop.

Papier-mâché pulp is a very cheap type of modelling material. When pulped until it is a homogeneous mass it is ideal for making carved details. To make the pulp, newsprint is soaked overnight in warm-to-hot water and then put through a household mincing machine. (The same effect can be achieved by hand but this is very laborious.) The pulp is then squeezed to get rid of the surplus liquid, and formed into a nest shape. Hot, liquid glue size is added and mixed thoroughly. This is formed into the nest shape again and plaster of Paris added. The mixture is now very malleable and can be shaped by rolling it in the hands. It can now be used like modelling clay. When dry, papier-mâché pulp is rock hard and very strong.

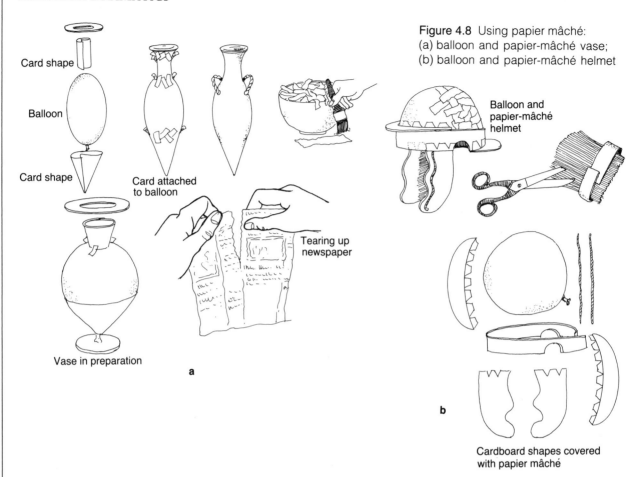

Figure 4.8 Using papier mâché:
(a) balloon and papier-mâché vase;
(b) balloon and papier-mâché helmet

Card shape

Balloon

Card shape

Card attached
to balloon

Tearing up
newspaper

Vase in preparation

a

Balloon and
papier-mâché
helmet

b

Cardboard shapes covered
with papier mâché

Painted with the correct paints it will even withstand water.

Plaster of Paris

Plaster of Paris is another useful medium for the props maker. It is advisable to use finer, refined, dental plaster as this gives a better finish and is tougher than the coarse, builder's type of plaster. Basically, plaster of Paris can be used with many other materials. Scrim and gauze soaked in plaster can be draped around a framework to give it additional texture. Plaster of Paris is particularly useful in making moulds. This process is explained later in this chapter.

An example of modelling

As an example of modelling, the first project might be the production of a bust or head—perhaps a dismembered head or bust of one of the characters. This may seem an impossible task without the help of a sculptor, but with a

very limited knowledge of modelling this can be achieved. A tin of CA37 alginate elastic-impression compound should be bought from a dental supplier. Although expensive, this is the quickest and simplest way of making a life mask, and full instructions are included in each tin. When mixed, this is a malleable substance that can be applied over the face with a pliable spatula. It should always be mixed in small quantities because of its quick-drying ability. The colder the water used, the longer will be the setting time. It is easier if two people work together, one mixing while the other applies the ready-mixed substance. This mixture sets into a rubber-like compound capable of reproducing the finest detail. It is ready for use as a mould in minutes of being removed from the face. Because of its rubberiness there are no problems of undercuts. There are drawbacks to it as its life-span is very short, and a plaster cast has to be taken within a short time of making the mould as it soon loses its flexibility and can break up. However, this is a minor drawback when compared to the result that can be obtained.

Other materials for this project (apart from the face of the willing player!) are a plastic straw for the mouth, petroleum jelly, a plastic shoulder cape or towel, a plaster-impregnated bandage (or scrim dipped in a dental-plaster mixture), a flexible or plastic bowl of water, a table or bench, an old nylon stocking or tights (to cover the player's hair), a pliable spatula, scissors, and a brush.

The player is laid on the table or bench so that the technician can easily move around to reach all sides of the head. The hair is completely covered with the nylon stocking, and the straw placed in the mouth (see Figure 4.9). The face should be given a light coating of petroleum jelly, especially the eyelashes and eyebrows (it is inadvisable to cast the face of anyone who has a moustache or unduly long sideburns or a beard. Heavily whiskered faces would ruin the mould). Check that the hair to the hairline is covered with the nylon stocking. Facial tissues or gauze can act as a further

protection over the eyebrows, lashes, and any side hair.

With the player covered to the neck with the shoulder cape, the mould making can begin. The alginate (made up in small quantities) is applied to the face. The nostrils should not be covered—modelling round them is quite sufficient. If the instructions already given are followed carefully, the mask will be done quickly without any undue discomfort. It is important that the player does not move his or her face during the process, as this could distort the mould.

The cast should be allowed to dry for a few minutes, and then the impregnated plaster bandaging wetted and placed over it (or strips of gauze dipped into plaster of Paris). This acts as support, making the mould stronger and rigid, and keeping it in shape. The mould is removed (when dry) by stretching the face skin back at the side of the face to allow the air in. The straw is removed from the mouth, the mould slipped down towards the chin, and then off. A negative mould should have been formed.

Fill the flexible plastic bowl with sufficient water to fill the mould's face cavity. Sprinkle

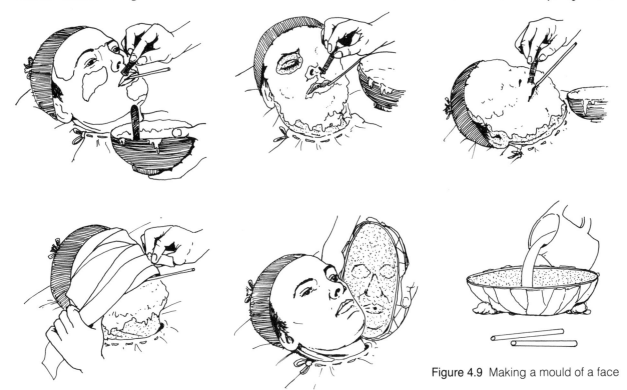

Figure 4.9 Making a mould of a face

113

plaster of Paris into the water until it reaches to just below water level. Then begin to stir. The best results are obtained with the hands, ensuring there are no lumps in the mixture whatsoever and that a creamy substance has been created. Then commence the pouring. Do not pour directly into the mould but down the side against the wall, allowing the plaster to flow to its own level. A slow continuous pour will help to expel most of the air and prevent any air bubbles from forming. Before allowing the plaster to set, place two 6 × ½ in (15 × 1.25 cm) pieces of dowelling in the mould about 5 in (12.5 cm) apart, leaving about 4 in (10 cm) protruding. This is to make a key for the clay in the front half of the modelled head. Allow the plaster to set completely and then remove the plaster-positive face mask (Figure 4.10(a)). Check for air bubbles. If present, a little wet plaster rubbed into the holes will get rid of them. The face impression complete, the top and back of the head must now be considered. Whether the head will be covered by a wig or whether it will be in the form of a bust, the process is the same—the only difference is the shoulders of a bust. The armature required for a bust is larger than that required for a head. The model's base is generally a stout piece of wood. This should be battened on its underside with two cross members to prevent any warping (Figure 4.10(b)). The modelling board should then be placed on a stand, about 1 m high from the ground (Figure 4.10(c)). The equipment needed for modelling is as follows (Figure 4.10(d)): three or four spatulas of various sizes; one medium-sized spatula with

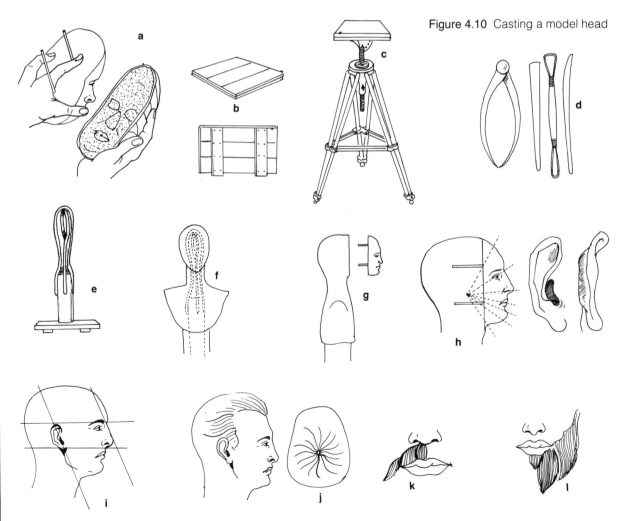

Figure 4.10 Casting a model head

strong wire curves at the ends; a pair of callipers; one medium-sized flexible bowl; two metal spatulas for cleaning the mould; one 2.5-cm chisel; and a quantity of superfine dental plaster. The best source of light is a top light set at an angle of about 45°. A small sponge will be needed to keep the hands clean during the modelling process, and a sheet of polythene to cover the work to keep it damp if it is left for a day. A fine water spray (a garden spray) or a wet brush will also help to keep the clay moist. The clay should be kneaded and worked through the hands to make it pliable.

In the centre of the modelling board, place an upright piece of wood about 9 in (23 cm) high and about 2 in (5 cm) square (if the model is to be just the head). This should be firmly attached to the base. A length of lead piping is then nailed to the upright (to reach the top of the head; for the bust, use strong piping). Lead piping is very malleable, should the bust's head's direction need to be changed during the modelling process (Figure 4.10(e)). Over this piping, chicken wire twisted and moulded to a rough head shape is placed, or a soft wire armature (a square, aluminium, section wire is most commonly used). Either method should stop the heavy, wet clay collapsing.

When the framework is complete, wet the board and armature thoroughly and then lay a good coating of clay all over it. The clay should not be applied too thickly—if it is it will be necessary to remove some of the clay afterwards to achieve the head's natural bulk. Layers should be added progressively. Begin modelling at the neck and then up to the top of the head (Figure 4.10(f)). Now take the plaster mask and fix it securely into the clay, pressing the protruding dowelling in firmly (Figure 4.10(g)). With small pellets of clay, bring the plaster face in to line with the mass of the head. Ask the player whose head is being modelled to stand next to the clay model so that his or her head is level with the model. Make sure the player holds his or head as straight and as upright as possible, regardless of the eventual pose the head will be fashioned into. This will help you (along with the callipers) to obtain the

correct proportions and measurements. Measure the distance from ear to ear and mark these on the model by placing a matchstick into the clay. The ears should be (horizontally) at the same level. The ears must be in the correct position with regard to all other features: the position of the ears is the central point from which all other distances are measured—forehead, nose, mouth, and chin (Figure 4.10(h)). Placing the ears too far from the nose will make the head appear too small; likewise, if the ears are too far forward the head will appear flat. The top line of the ears should be in line with the arch of the eyebrow; the base of the ears should be in line with the nostrils or the tip of the nose (Figure 4.10(i)). (There are alternatives, but these positions seem to be the general rule.) Study the contours of the ear, back and front, and notice the distance from the head and the general contours of the ear.

Having decided on the ears' position, the head's pose can now be struck. Take hold of the head with both hands, placing them very carefully behind the ears but without touching them and, with gentle but firm pressure, turn the head in whatever direction is required.

Next comes the modelling of the hair (if a wig is not going to be used instead). Hair is modelled in the following stages (Figure 4.10(j)): the front from the centre of the face; the temples; the section below the temples at the sides; and the top of the hair, which grows from a central point—the crown—and from which the hair fans out in all directions. To accentuate the hair on a bust, detailed, deep curves suggest dark hair, and less detail lighter hair. If the player is to have a moustache or beard, this must be added to the model. The moustache grows on each side of the face in three distinct sections (Figure 4.10(k)). The first section is attached below the nostrils, the second to the upper lip, and the third to the cheek. A beard is very similar to hair, but study the beard very carefully as its colour can vary from the hair colouring (Figure 4.10(l)).

Model the hair as carefully as possible: badly constructed hair can spoil the entire effect of an otherwise good head. Too much or too little detail can detract from the mask taken from the player's face. The details should never be the most apparent features—they should add interest and harmonize the head's 'colour' and character, accentuating the surfaces that mark off the different features. You should also bear in mind that, wherever it is placed under stage lighting, it must always retain its resemblance to the features and character of the player.

For a severed-head effect (Figure 4.11(a)), the model is now finished (the methods of casting and painting are given later). The lower part of the bust (the shoulders), however, should be modelled in clay (Figure 4.11(b)) or shaped in chicken wire over which a stiffish felt that has been dipped in glue size is moulded into the shape of a cloak or uniform, etc. (Figure 4.11(c)). When this is completely dry, it is covered with a coat of soapy or clay water and it is now ready for casting. The plaster mask should be given three coats of shellac (allowing each to dry before the next is applied). This will give the mask a hard outer covering (Figure 4.11(d)). Over this is applied a layer of soap or separating gelatine to prevent it from sticking to the plaster mould. This, too, is now ready for casting.

The model having been completed, the plaster of Paris model can now be made (the bust should be divided into sections for easier casting). As the model head will eventually be made in latex, this will reduce the problem of undercutting: the model head need only be divided into two parts (to create a two-piece mould). The division between the two parts can be made in two ways: with bands of clay or

Figure 4.11 Modelling a head or bust

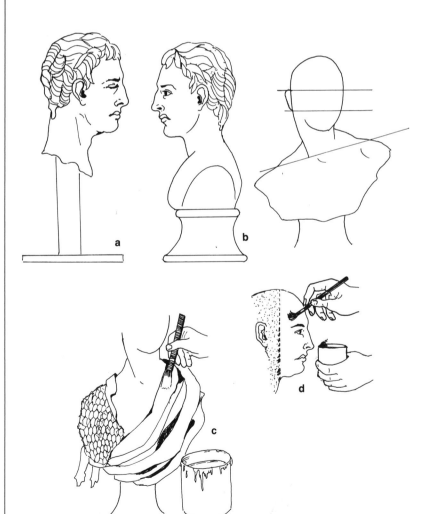

116

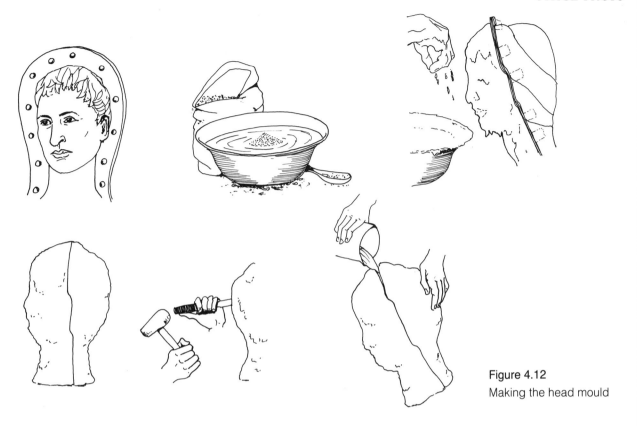

Figure 4.12
Making the head mould

metal pegs. The metal pegs are butted and overlapped to prevent plaster seepage, and placed in a zig-zag pattern. The clay division is made from a band of clay, 1½ in (4 cm) wide and about ¼ in (0.6 cm) thick. This is made as follows (Figure 4.12). Make a roll of clay 1 in (2.5 cm) thick and about 1 in (2.5 cm) long, according to the model's size. Put this band of clay on a board or a formica-topped kitchen table and beat it until it is absolutely flat (about ¼ in (0.6 cm) thick). Smooth it out with a small glass jar or bottle, and then cut it lengthways with a knife to a width of 1¼ in (3 cm). Now lay it along the top of the head and down the sides, so that the bust is divided into two parts, front and back, from the centre of the head. Push the boundary clay down the sides of the head ½ in (1.25 cm) behind the ears and curving in to drop down the sides of the neck to the base. Make sure the back section is slightly narrower than the front. The boundary must be firm but must not disturb the head, and there must be no gaps between the boundary and the model. The boundary can be

further secured with small supports of clay. Indent the boundary at regular intervals to make keys that will allow the second half of the mould to fit snugly and neatly to the first. Cover the back of the bust with a sheet of plastic or moistened paper to prevent liquid plaster, when it is thrown, from falling on the half of the mould.

Make up the plaster of Paris as described earlier for the mask—remember to make only sufficient at a time to work with, otherwise it will harden in the bowl before it can be applied. It is advisable to place newspaper or other covering on the work table and surrounding floor during the next operation. Hold the container of plaster in one hand and, with the other, scoop out a handful of plaster. With the back of the hand held towards the model, throw the plaster from the tips of the fingers. Enough force must be exerted to ensure that the plaster penetrates the finest detailed crevices. However, plaster of Paris expands slightly on setting, which further ensures penetration.

The first layer of plaster should be about

½ in (1.25 cm) thick and, at this stage, should still reveal the shape of the model. As this first layer begins to set it should be roughened gently, either with a spatula or with the fingers. Small lumps of loose plaster can be pushed in to make the surface as rough as possible to form a key for the second layer.

Prepare the second layer of plaster in the same way as the first but this mixture can be left a little longer before being applied. Throw the plaster on as before, and repeat the process until the full thickness of plaster has been achieved at the top of the clay boundary. This brings the thickness up to the necessary 1½ in (4 cm), which will be able to carry the weight of the piece. When the first half of the mould has completely set, the clay boundaries are removed with the plastic sheet or moistened paper.

Before starting on the second half, make sure the keys are clearly indented in the plaster, that there are no air holes, and that the wall is reasonably smooth. If the keys are not clearly defined, take the metal spatula and penetrate the plaster about ¼ in (0.6 cm) to create an indent with a 1-in (2.5-cm) wide funnel shape. Air holes can be filled with moistened plaster. The walls can be smoothed by scraping them with the metal spatula. All these repairs must be carried out without disturbing the other half of the model. The plaster boundary should now be washed lightly with soapy water, detergent, or even a thin, clay-water wash, to prevent plaster sticking to plaster. Check for any damage to the clay half of the model, which should be made good. Now make the second half of the mould in exactly the same way.

After allowing the plaster to set overnight, the mould will be ready for opening. Take a 1-in (2.5-cm) chisel and gently prise the two halves apart all the way round. On no account use force, as this could damage or break it. Through this opening, allow a little water (about half a cupful) to run in between the clay and the plaster. This will cause the clay to expand and hence push the two halves apart.

Detach one half of the mould from the clay (the other piece will still be attached). Remove

Figure 4.13 Pouring latex into the mould

the clay by gently digging it out with the fingers until all traces of the clay model have been removed. Gently prise the mask out of the mould. It should come away easily as it has been treated not to stick to the plaster. If there are any crevices that cannot be reached with the brush, use a small modelling tool.

With warm water, thoroughly clean the mould until all traces of clay have gone. Leave the two halves to dry out. As the casting is to be in latex, the mould's surface will not need any further treatment. If, however, the mould is to be made of laminated paper mâché (as described earlier) the procedure will be different. The dry mould is given three coats of thin shellac varnish or button polish on its internal surface to prevent absorption. It is then lightly smeared with a thin coat of Vaseline before the papier mâché is laid.

As already mentioned, for latex composition the mould is left untreated. The mould is first re-assembled, making sure the keys fit comfortably. The mould is then bound together with a strong cord to ensure an even closer fit. Turn the mould over so that its bottom is uppermost (Figure 4.13). Balance the mould at an angle of 45° (a wedge-shaped piece of wood is ideal for this). The liquid latex and filler paste should be mixed in roughly equal parts, but the more filler paste, the harder the finished model. The mixture should be allowed to stand for a while to remove any air bubbles that may have formed while mixing. When the mixture is ready, pour a little into the mould. Even though the mould is somewhat heavy, it should be rocked to and fro to allow the latex to run round the seams or joining lines of the mould. After a few minutes the mould should be emptied of any surplus of this small amount of latex (that will have sealed all cracks and joints) and then the mould should be filled completely with the liquid latex solution. A little knock now and then during pouring will help the latex to reach all parts. Allow the mixture to remain in the mould for up to one hour. During this time, keep an eye on the liquid as it falls to its own level. Top up if necessary. After an hour, the mould is inverted and the residue is poured back into the container. The mould should now be left to dry in a warm atmosphere, allowing the latex to mature naturally.

After twenty-four hours the cord should be carefully untied and the two halves dismantled. Once released from the mould, the latex model bust should be given a further drying period. A shrinkage of about 10 per cent takes place from the original clay model, but this will be quite unnoticeable to the audience. Finish off the model by removing the flash line around the seam with either a heated, sharp, metal knife and then fine sandpaper or with an electric buffer. The severed head can be painted and 'made up' in the same way as the player. The bust can be given a coat of off-white scenic paint to give it a marble effect. Latex is perfect for painting, and will take most oil and acrylic paints (Figure 4.14).

Liquid latex also makes very realistic skin: it can be used as make-up to give natural-looking wrinkles. Produced by the plaster-mould method, such items as light-weight armour, face masks, and helmets can also be made. Other parts of the body (hands, feet, etc.) can also be reproduced in this way.

Vinamold

Vinamold hot-melting compound—although quite expensive—has many advantages: it is very adaptable (similar to alginate) but has the added bonus of being more durable and

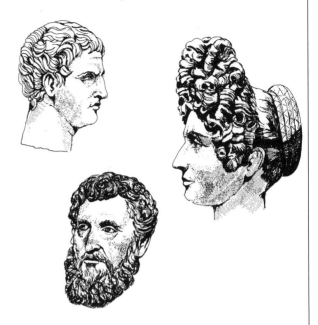

Figure 4.14 Finished models

reusable. Like alginate, it will recreate undercuts and fine detail, and is therefore very useful when large quantities of replicas are required. It will reproduce almost any original from any material: plaster, clay, wood, Plasticine, glass, metal, and china.

Before using this compound, the manufacturer's instructions should be read thoroughly; however, the following steps generally apply. The original item or model should be fastened securely to prevent it floating up in the hot Vinamold. A retaining vessel for the Vinamold must be made, and the simplest method is to form thick, oiled paper or a sheet of thin metal into a cylinder and to secure this with string. Clay or Plasticine should be pressed around the base of the cylinder to prevent the compound from seeping out.

Depending on the quantities involved, a hot-air crucible or (for smaller quantities) an aluminium or stainless steel saucepan can be used as a melting-pot. The Vinamold is cut into very small pieces, and a handful is placed into the melting-pot over a moderate heat. The compound must be stirred constantly until all the pieces have melted; more pieces can then be added until the required quantity is reached. When the Vinamold is completely liquid, the melting-pot must be removed from the heat and allowed to cool to around 120°C.

When this temperature has been reached, the compound should be poured as quickly as possible and in one constant, even stream. At no point should the hot liquid be poured directly over the model itself but between the model and the retaining cylinder or down the cylinder's walls. As the mixture rises from the bottom, it forces the air from the finer details of the model. Before removing the model, several hours must elapse to allow the compound to cool.

When the Vinamold has set, the model can be removed from the now-flexible mould by slitting it open with a sharp craft knife. The flexible mould obtained should either be bound with wire or tape or, if it will be used constantly or over a long run, a two-piece plaster case should be made for it (this was explained under the plaster-mould section).

If certain props have to be broken at every performance, plaster models are ideal for these. With the mould secure in its outer plaster case and bound with string or strong elastic bands, it is turned bottom up. Liquid plaster is then poured in, as explained earlier. After waiting for about twenty minutes, untie the mould, remove the outer casing, retie the mould halves, and then pour in plaster for the next reproduction.

Fibreglass models can also be made from Vinamold but, although fibreglass is very useful, most of the materials connected with its use can be hazardous. If there is a call for fibreglass props, contact a fibreglass manufacturer, who will explain the correct procedure: there is a high risk of fire as well as a health hazard.

Cold-curing rubber

Because of its heat-resisting and negligible-shrinking qualities, cold-cure silicone rubber is ideal for preparing moulds for making metal and plastic props, and it can be bought at most good art stores. The rubber compound is mixed with a catalyst (or curing agent) supplied with the compound. This catalyst either accelerates or retards the curing time, according to the manufacturer's instructions (which must be followed very carefully).

The article to be modelled is placed on a Plasticine base, which will hold it down and prevent it from floating away when the silicone is poured in. The retaining walls are made in the same way as for Vinamold: a thin, cylindrical, metal sheet secured with string or wire. The bottom of the retaining wall is made fast with Plasticine.

Mix the solutions according to the manufacturer's instructions, taking care not to trap air bubbles that will turn into holes. Mixing can take about ten minutes, depending on room temperature and the amount of curing agent used. (Curing time begins the moment the two solutions come together, and the normal time for full curing is roughly forty-eight hours.)

When the mixing is complete, pouring commences. As with Vinamold, the liquid must be poured down the side of the retaining wall or between the model and the wall—never directly onto the model itself. Again, the pouring should be in one steady flow; if, however, there are deep undercuts on the original, it is as well to brush some of the mixture on these parts *before* pouring. This will eliminate any chance of air bubbles forming. When the silicone rubber has cured (in forty-eight hours), remove the surrounding wall. The original will be completely encased in a solid, cylindrical, rubber shape.

With a felt-tip pen, mark a line vertically around the rubber mould to give the halfway mark for the plaster casing. However, make certain this line does not cross any important detail otherwise, when slit, the casting or seal line will destroy the effect. Prepare a bed of clay and embed the rubber mould in up to the felt-tip mark. Roughen the rubber outer moulding and make indentations so that the plaster will have a key. A clay-retaining wall should be built around the clay bed and the embedded rubber mould, with a rough space of about 1 in (2.5 cm) all round. Make up the plaster of Paris as previously, and fill the mould to the height of the retaining wall. When dry, reverse the mould, remove the clay bed, cover the plaster surface with soapy water or detergent, and allow it to dry. Build a further retaining wall and repeat the process. When dry, remove the plaster casing and place the silicone rubber mould on a flat surface. Slit down the centre marking line with a sharp craft knife. This mark shows the dividing plaster line and also the cut-line for extracting the original.

Open the rubber mould, remove the original, replace the rubber mould into one half of the plaster casting, and scrape out a conical shape from the rubber mould. Repeat this process with the other half. There should now be a continuous pour-hole through the plaster outer casing and the rubber mould that gives an accurate impression of the original. Before assembling the mould, a light dusting of graphite powder will aid the reproduction of high-quality metal castings. Replace the rubber mould and plaster casing, bind with string or elastic bands, and the mould is now ready for casting. Place the mould at a 45° angle for easier pouring and gradually straighten it up to allow the metal to find its own level.

Metal casting

Follow the manufacturer's instructions when using polyester-resin, rigid-laminating compounds. If the casting is to be in metal, a good-quality metal ladle is the only piece of equipment required. The choice of metal or alloy is best left to an experienced person, but generally a low-melting alloy is easier to handle and better if slight movement is required in the object.

The silicone mould should be bound securely and placed on a bench. The low-melting alloy should be placed in the ladle and heated until liquid. Correct timing is essential—the alloy's silvery surface begins to turn a bluish brown when it is ready.

Pouring must be done gradually and carefully, a few drops at a time. Allow a few minutes for the metal to solidify and then start to remove the casting (residual heat in the mould can damage it). Always remove the model using long-nosed pliers, applying a gentle easing and rocking motion.

Sand casting

Another method for casting metal or plaster is the old one of sand casting. Although not used much today, this process is still useful. Sand is placed in a container and levelled off. It is then moistened with water and oil, and allowed to settle. The model is pressed into the wet sand and carefully removed, leaving its impression undamaged. The metal or plaster is then slowly poured into the impression. When cool or dry, it is loosened by drawing a knife or other sharp implement around its edge and then removed.

The sand is levelled again, moistened, the original pressed in, and the whole process repeated. Although slow, this method of casting is ideal for small items, such as medallions, and for relief-work types of props.

Polystyrene and polyurethane foam

Expanded polystyrene is versatile, light, resembles firm plastic, and is solid so that it can be easily carved by hand or machine. It can be bought in 8 × 4 ft (2.5 × 1 m) blocks that can be carved with a knife or by heat.

When using a knife, a long, narrow-bladed, flexible craft type is best, which must always be kept very sharp. Alternatively, a home-made knife, such as a honed and ground hacksaw blade with a handle, will serve as well. Because of the nature of the material, carving should be done patiently: a little at a time, finished off with fine sandpaper.

When pieces have to be joined or strengthened, wooden dowels can be inserted and glued together (however, take care when choosing adhesives: some tend to soften polystyrene, and some form a tough skin that is difficult to sand down). To give polystyrene a smooth surface, paint it with emulsion and, when dry, rub it down with wet-and-dry sandpaper.

Fire regulations must be observed when using large pieces of polystyrene—cover them with a fireproof material, such as muslin or cheese-cloth, before painting them. Props made of polystyrene can also be covered with latex and cloth, which hardens the surface and protects it from damage.

Latex and cloth can also be used to achieve

such effects as tree bark, stumps, logs, and trunks. To create a coarse, tree-bark effect, strips of cloth can be entwined with each other and then fastened to the polystyrene. They are then coated with a latex solution.

Polyurethane foam plastic is also useful. Two plastic compounds are mixed together that foam to several times their original volume before they set. These can be bought in either flexible or rigid forms. A wide variety of realistic props (bread, meat, fish, suckling pigs, roasted poultry, etc.) can be made from this material. Larger props, such as pillars, can also be constructed by using a wooden frame. A balloon is held firmly in a mould until it has been filled, foamed-up and set; then the balloon skin is removed, leaving a round or sausage shape with a smooth outer surface. Polyurethane foam plastic is ideal for 'packing-out' castings made in liquid latex. However, care should be taken that not too much foam is inserted as it exerts great pressure and could distort the rubber casting.

MISCELLANEOUS EFFECTS

Cobwebs

Ghostly or dingy interiors can be achieved by convincing trailing cobwebs. These are very fragile and take some time to prepare but are worth it for the effect they create. There are two types of cobweb: fine filaments of terylene or glass, or filaments of rubber spun from a cobweb 'gun'. Terylene or glass cobwebs can be purchased in hanks for dressing the set as required. However, rubber cobwebs are more effective, especially if the players have to grope their way through them. These adhere to anything and, given time, can be renewed for each performance.

The cobweb 'gun' is a hand-held device with an electric motor that rotates a fan blade and a cup containing liquid-latex solution. The fan blade and cup are mounted in line directly on the motor's spindle, so the cobwebs can thus be sprayed directly onto the set ('guns' are available for hire).

To give cobwebs their full effect, dust them with talcum powder or fuller's earth. Place some powder on the palm of the hand and then gently blow it over the cobwebs.

Breakable props

In real life, a china vase, when dropped, will shatter. On the stage, however, the chances are that, when one of the players has to recreate such an effect, the vase will bounce and roll away. To avoid such embarrassment, the props department should be well versed in making breakable items.

Simulated glass is difficult to achieve: it must be tough enough to handle and yet fragile enough to shatter on cue. Sugar glass (a type of toffee) has been used for some time but, apart from tasting good, it has many disadvantages. It is easily broken and can cut. Other simple and economic materials can now be bought in sheets to make breakable bottles, vases, and cups that will perform in every way like the real article but will shatter naturally without harming the performer.

The simplest material is wax cast in plaster moulds. The mould is moistened thoroughly, filled and swilled with hot, molten paraffin wax, and, within seconds, emptied. This process is repeated until the casting is of a near-uniform thickness.

Never allow the wax at the base of a wax bottle to settle or become too thick: in a fight scene an unfortunate player could receive a nasty blow, often without the bottle breaking. It is advisable to drain the mould upside down after each pouring and swilling to ensure an overall thickness. After being cast, the wax can be lightly painted and a label attached to it (Figure 4.15(a)).

Vases can be cast in wax and decorated. They can also be filled with flowers and water to add realism when broken. Bottles and vases can also be made of plaster, and the same process as for wax should be followed. The plaster is again poured into the mould and swilled around to create a thin shell. Plaster props should be broken by a sharp bang down on the head or whatever—never by a thrust as

Figure 4.15 Props effects:
(a) exploding bottle; (b) log fire;
(c) exploding doorway; (d) pea tray;
(e) wind machine; (f) thunder sheet

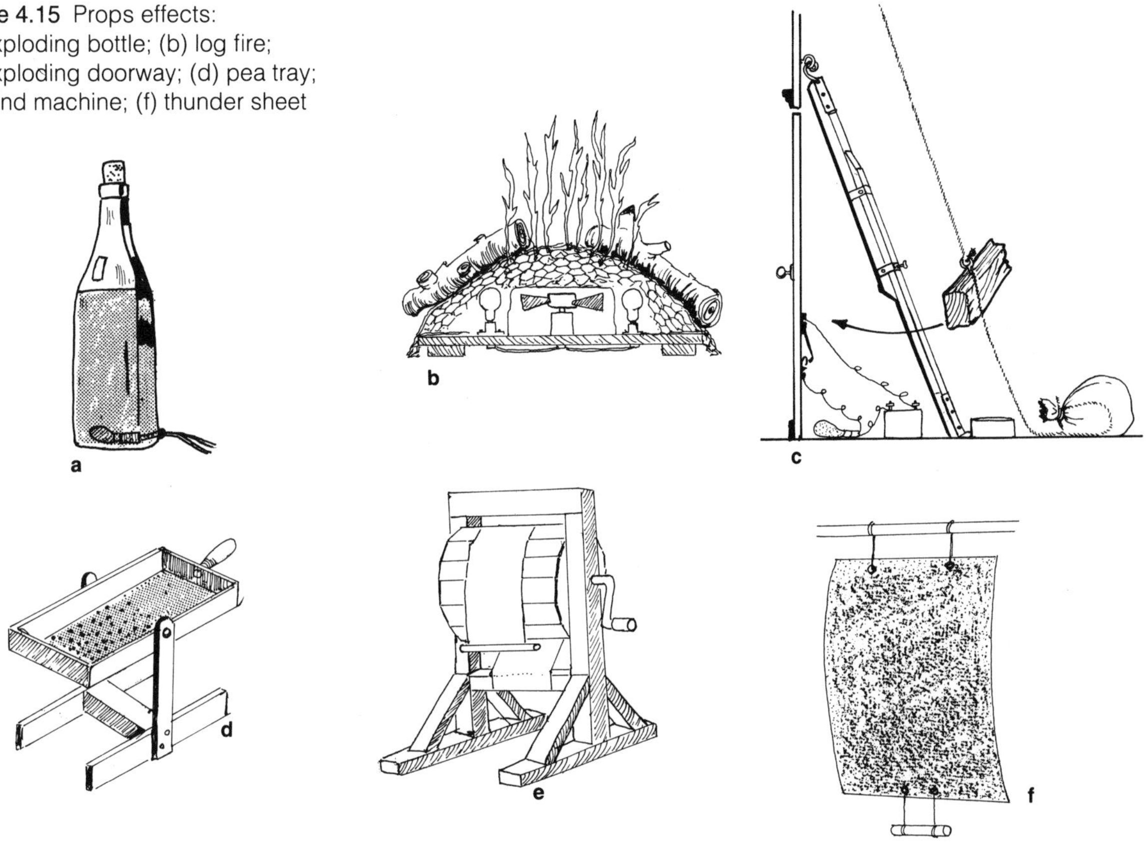

the greater rigidity in its broken edges could cut.

If a scene calls for a bullet to shatter a vase or bottle, a small pyro-fuse and a small capsule of flash powder can be placed in it close to one of its walls. If the vessel is half filled with water this increases the pressure when it is electrically detonated and, when exploded, a wide-spread destructive effect is achieved.

Furniture that has to be broken can be made entirely of balsa wood. If so, nails and screws must never be used in its construction. Instead, saw cuts should be made in the furniture and the player rehearsed to know that the cuts open on a downward stroke but close on an upward one. If such a prop is handled too energetically, it will fall apart in mid-air over the player's head.

Fire and smoke effects

Many special effects can be used by the props department in their search for realism, and most of these will involve working in partnership with a competent electrician (and unless one is available, many of the effects mentioned should not be used). Alternatively, effects can be hired, in which case the manufacturer's instructions must be followed very carefully.

Open log fires are easily constructed with chicken wire, plaster, or papier-mâché logs, and strips of silk ribbon, underneath which is placed a small electric fan and coloured lamps (Figure 4.15(b)). If smoke is required, smoke pellets or capsules are available that are capable of giving off small amounts of smoke. These are very quick burning and last only about thirty seconds. For longer periods, charcoal tablets (as used in incense burners in churches) are more effective. Composed of compressed charcoal and treated with a chemical to aid ignition, these glow when alight but do not as yet smoke. A few drops of oil placed on their surface produces smoke, which will last for up to half an hour. Hence they can be lit and positioned before the smoke is needed and are therefore useful for fireplaces, stoves, etc. They are available in a box-kit form.

To simulate a conflagration, the set can be lit with the flickering effects caused by a flame drum. This can be made quite simply. Take a length of black paper, 1 ft (30 cm) wide and 6 ft (2 m) long, and slit it along its entire length in various ways (diagonally, wavy) up to 1 in (2.5 cm) from either side. Join the paper end to end to create a cylinder and seal the end with circles of hardboard to form a drum.

There are many ways of operating this. A spindle can be attached and the drum turned by hand or a length of cord can be fastened to it, rotated until wound tight, and then allowed to spin freely. Either way, a lamp is positioned behind the drum and the cut-out slits (passing in front of the lamp) give the effect of flickering flames. Two or more drums produce a random pattern that is more realistic than a repetitive one. Bellowing smoke completes the effect.

For pantomime-genie effects, the safest method is the flash pot, which consists of a container of flash powder that, when ignited, gives off a bright flash and a cloud of smoke but no explosive noise. Flash pots are also known as stage flashes or mag-puffs. To create an explosive bang, small maroons are usually ignited at the same time.

Explosions

Another special effect that has a dramatic impact on an audience is blowing out a door or wall. This is achieved by using a swinging-weight method (Figure 4.15(c)). A weighted object is released that has been suspended above and behind the set. As it swings it clears anything in its way. The weight can be disguised as a wooden beam shaped like a box to hold the weight or sand. The door or wall must be free of hinges or fastenings, and the weight should be positioned to strike the door or wall at its base.

To stop the weight swinging forward, a stop line should be attached to the weight and to another weighted object or sandbag. The placing of this second weight is crucial, as it determines the drag before the swinging weight stops. A flash battery can be situated just behind the door and, at the moment of impact, this will fill the door area with smoke (which will also help to conceal the swinging weight).

Iron bars

Bendable metal or iron bars (prison bars) are nothing more than rubber tubing covering with a soft aluminium rod. Ornate ironwork can be made by casting latex over a soft wire core. Melting metal is made from a model made in paraffin wax with metal-powder filling.

Dry ice

Chemicals can be used in many ways to produce special effects, and books written for school experiments or amateur illusionists are well worth researching. Foaming drinks can be achieved by placing a small piece of dry ice in water, which will cause it to bubble rapidly and give off 'smoke'. Although this can be drunk, it is inadvisable to allow dry ice to enter the mouth. Sugar has the same effect when dropped into a fizzy drink. The sugar causes a release of carbon dioxide, again producing a quick-foaming effect.

Dream sequences, low-lying mists, boggy marshlands, and docksides are simulated by a dry-ice machine. Dry-ice clouds, which are heavy and cold, need retaining walls at the sides of the stage—narrow scenic flats are ideal to keep the clouds in position. Previously, these machines were made by the props department but they are now widely available for sale or hire. They can be wheeled about backstage without any problem.

Manual sound effects

Sound effects are usually created on tape and hence come under the responsibility of the lighting or electrics department. However, many effects can be achieved by other means: wind can be simulated by a voice softly moaning or whistling through a microphone; and dried peas slowly rolled around on a drum create a good rain effect (Figure 4.15(d)—applause can be achieved in the same manner).

Figure 4.16 Swords and spears

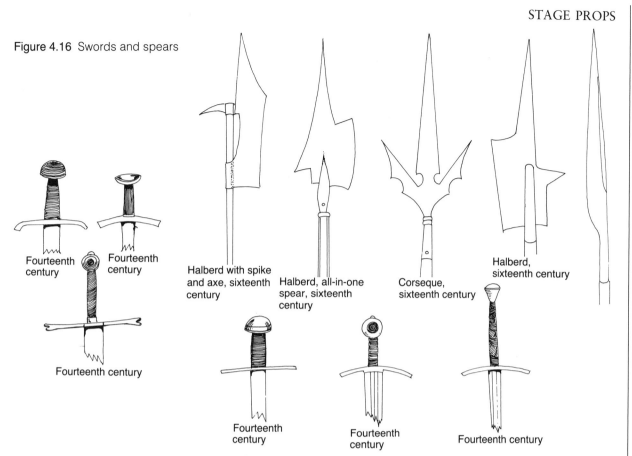

Fourteenth century

Fourteenth century

Fourteenth century

Halberd with spike and axe, sixteenth century

Halberd, all-in-one spear, sixteenth century

Corseque, sixteenth century

Halberd, sixteenth century

Fourteenth century

Fourteenth century

Fourteenth century

Figure 4.17 Shields and helmets

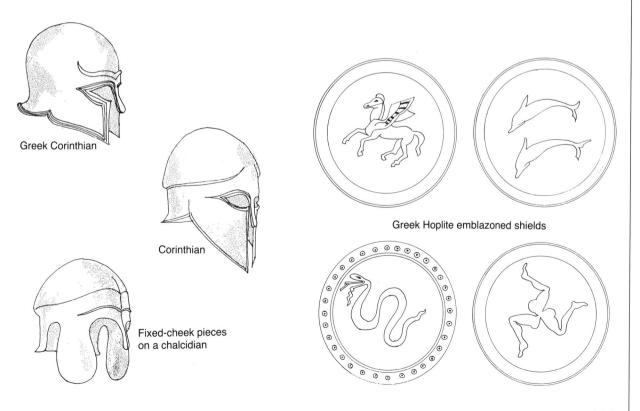

Greek Corinthian

Corinthian

Fixed-cheek pieces on a chalcidian

Greek Hoplite emblazoned shields

(Figure 4.15(e) shows a wind machine.)

Rolling thunder is effectively simulated by hanging a thin metal sheet (1 m by 1.25 m) freely from a beam. Hold one corner with the hand and gently and slowly shake it with the other. As the rattle starts, shake it a little faster to create a rumbling sound (Figure 4.15(f)).

Crowd noises are best achieved by people shouting things relevant to the play off stage. Battle noises are achieved similarly, only with the addition of drumming and the occasional bang and clash of steel.

To create the effect of breaking glass, place two galvanized metal buckets off stage, one full of broken glass and the other empty. On cue, pour the glass from one bucket into the other.

Crowns and jewellery

Crowns and jewellery, etc., can be made from many of the techniques discussed in this chapter. Figure 4.18 gives suggested crown shapes.

Weapons

Most theatrical stores stock non-practical weapons: daggers with blades that retract into the handle, look-alike guns, and so forth. Period firearms are usually hired from theatrical-supply gunsmiths, and these can be fired by igniting a loose powder charge outside the barrel. Others fire blank cartridges. All weapons should be treated with great respect. Many weapons can also be made by the props department (see Figures 4.16, 4.17 and 4.19).

Figure 4.18 Crowns

Figure 4.19 Firearms: (a) prop guns can be made with shaped wooden stocks according to the period; (b) barrels can be made from any metal piping or 2.5 cm dowelling; (c) cleaning rods can be made with 0.6 cm dowelling; (d) trigger guards and flintlocks can be made up of any odd pieces of plastic or metal. The pistol barrel (e) can also be made from piping or dowelling. The stock of the pistol (f) can be made from wood for the period required, and trigger guards (g) can be made from metal or plastic

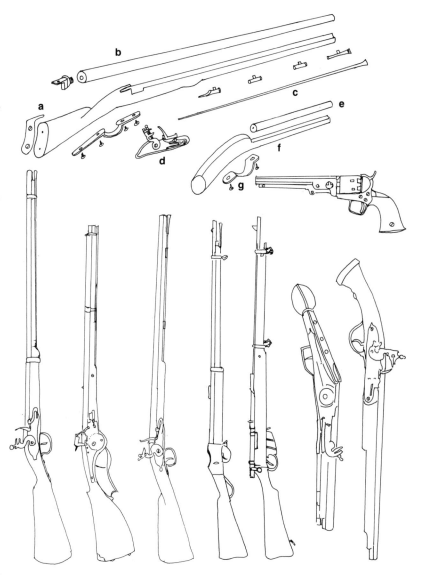

5

Lighting and sound effects

INTRODUCTION

From earliest times to the nineteenth century, light was merely used to enable the audience to see the players and lighting effects were virtually unknown. Greek and Roman theatres depended on daylight; medieval theatres used candles, blazing pine knots in iron cressets, or open oil lamps with floating wicks for decorative purposes. However, the indoor theatres of sixteenth and seventeenth century created lighting problems. Open oil lamps were hung on brackets above the stage or placed along the front of the stage (precursors of the footlights that were to be used over the following centuries). To increase brilliance, reflectors were installed, but as each lamp had to be lit individually, this was time consuming and also a great fire hazard. The eighteenth century saw the introduction of glass covers, which decreased the fire risk and increased control of the lamps.

In the nineteenth century, candles and oil lamps were still in use but, in 1817, the Drury Lane theatre was lit entirely by gas light operated by a man at a gas table—the prototype of the modern switchboard. Towards the end of the nineteenth century, the incandescent electric lamp was introduced. The techniques of lighting and electrically operated sound now took their rightful places with other facets of theatre art.

Stage lighting is used to complement costume, props, and set, and without it, the whole visual effect of the production would be much poorer, perhaps even lost. Lighting is an essential part of the whole stage design: the careful and subtle blending of light and colour can produce many moods and atmospheres— far beyond the brush of the scenery painter. Any production, no matter how small or simple, can create a living picture with the minimum of lighting equipment.

SAFETY PRECAUTIONS

Of all facets of the theatre, lighting is probably the most dangerous and so, when choosing the lighting team, each member's knowledge and expertise should be taken into consideration. One of the director's or designer's main concerns is that all equipment should be checked, and all lights should be safely and securely fastened (Figure 5.1). All fire regulations should be observed rigidly. If you are in doubt about an electrical or lighting matter, check with the local fire officer. Nothing is more dangerous than an insecure light crashing down on performer and spectator alike.

Safe working practice extends further—when 'setting up' always work with the electrical power disconnected. Fasten down all cables and never leave them coiled up tightly as they will generate heat. If it is necessary to climb ladders, someone should steady and foot them.

PERIOD ATMOSPHERE

The historical period of the play should generally be followed to create the right atmosphere. Iron holders containing spluttering torches

Figure 5.1 Safety precautions:
(a) cable clove hitch for securing
cable to the spot bar; (b) safety
clamp for hanging lamps

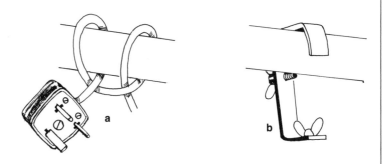

dipped in fat, or open bowls of burning oil were used from earliest times. In medieval days, the commonest form of lighting was the oil-burning cresset lamp made from stone or pottery and hung from the ceiling or wall. Poorer establishments had only rush lights, while richer ones had fine wax candles in candlesticks. Metal lanterns were hung from beams or stood on tables. These were cylindrical and contained a candle on a pricket spike. Later, copper and brass lanterns holding a candle and having a horn or a glass-panelled hinged door were introduced. These were hung from beams or placed on tables.

The nineteenth century saw candle-lit chandeliers, candelabra, and oil containers fitted with clockwork pumps. Homes in the early Victorian period continued to use the earlier lighting methods, but street lighting used gas. By 1840 gaslight became general for town houses and, from 1860, lighting was available by four different methods: gas, oil, candles, and electricity.

LIGHTING EQUIPMENT

Basic lamp designs have altered little over the years. What changes have occurred have mainly been the addition of such things as protective shielding, heat-protected adjusting knobs, and ventilation. Lanterns differ in shape and size and in the type and power of lamp (bulb) they can hold. To adjust a lantern finely, the correct lamp must be used. Quartz-halogen bulbs have largely superseded the incandescent type, but the latter are still in use.

The simplest lantern is the floodlight (Figure 5.2), which produces a large coverage of light and is used specifically for this. The cyclorama floodlight is basically the same as the floodlight and this is used to light a large vertical area, such as a backdrop. These floodlights are usually banked in rows at the top and bottom to give an even spread of colour across the whole area. It is important to be able to control the intensity of floodlights or the subtlety of the spotlights will be lost.

Figure 5.2 Floodlights: (a) an iris 1
cyclorama flood, 1,000 W, available
in an iris 4, four-colour unit;
(b) 150–200 W, available singly or in
banks of four to eight for battens
(which is eight times 150 W or, as
four to eight footlights, eight times
150 W)

Small floodlights are sometimes grouped together in battens—long metal boxes or troughs with floods in each compartment. These are usually hung above the stage on a bar. Identical troughs are also used at stage level, and these are called groundrows (not to be confused with small pieces of low scenery with the same name). Again, used chiefly to light skycloths or cycloramas, these should ideally be on three separate wiring circuits to allow for three-colour mixing (see the section on gels, later in this chapter). The three primary colours go to the bottom, and one primary blue, a deep orange, and a blue-green go to the top.

The use of these battens at the front of the stage (footlights or floats) has now largely gone with the introduction of spotlights situated in front of the stage, which are often called the front-of-house lights.

A lantern fitted with a lens system is called a spotlight. Lenses direct the light so it can be shaped and controlled. The width of the light beam can be altered by simply changing the distance between the lens and the lamp by means of a sliding tray mechanism in the lantern. Two different spots can be created: the profile (hard-edged spot) and the Fresnel (soft-edged spot). The profile (Figure 5.3(a)) is usually the main light source on a stage, and its focal range gives it a defined, hard-edged accuracy. It is fitted on four sides with shutters that can be moved into the light beam to alter its flow onto stage, from hard to softer images.

Near the shutter is a groove or slot—the objective slot—and into this a range of devices can be inserted. An iris will create various circular beams. A gobo (see Figure 5.6)—a cut-out pattern on a metal slide—will cast an image onto the stage (with the correct lens systems, a

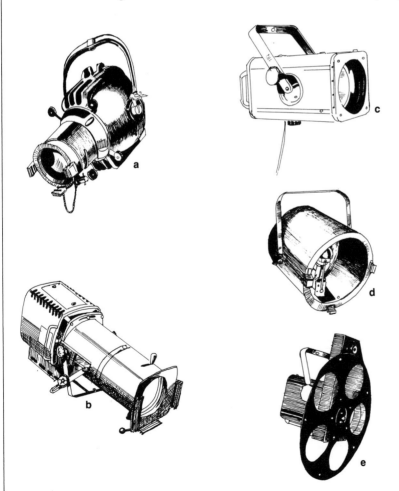

Figure 5.3 Types of lanterns: (a) profile spot, 500 W; (b) follow-spot with four-colour magazine; (c) Fresnel, 2,000 W; (d) beam light, 1,000 W; (e) colour-change wheel fitted with a remote control box and a thumb-wheel switch for each wheel. This allows for remote sequential access to any colour aperture or for continuous revolution. Available for two, four, or six wheels

gobo will be more effective, producing a hard focus in various sizes). A moving front-of-house spot is useful, as is a follow spot (Figure 5.3(b)) fitted with irises and a slide-over colour changer.

For larger areas of lighting, the Fresnel (Figure 5.3(c)) is used. Although this lacks many of the features of the profile, it gives a soft-edged beam in a variety of sizes. The only control over the light is by externally fitted doors (barn doors) that, however, do not harden the beam's edge (floodlights also create large areas of light, but floods cannot be altered in their size or shape). A Fresnel produces less light than a profile, and so its use is only apparent when it is close to the stage.

Other lanterns are available for specific jobs. The beam light (Figure 5.3(d)) has a very narrow spread; the Parcan (which has possibly taken over from the beam light) has narrow, medium, and wide beam angles. As these lanterns cannot be controlled they really offer very little for the amateur theatre. The PC spot was an attempt to improve the Fresnel, but its heavily frosted lens makes sharp definition impossible. Further lanterns can be obtained from theatrical electrical suppliers (e.g. colour wheel).

The director may want to use ultra-violet light. This is not expensive and, if used with discretion, can be very effective. It works only with the special fluorescent paints or specially prepared fabrics. All stage and front-of-house lights must be completely blacked out when using it, and white costumes or props, etc., should be avoided (unless it is intended that they should be seen) as these may pick up ultra violet. A glowing branding-iron for a torture scene can be made from fluorescent red plastic or other material painted with ultra-violet display paint and then spotlighted.

DESIGNING THE LIGHTING

The lanterns must be plugged into the mains and then connected to some form of control. For amateurs, this control will be a simple switchboard or dimmer. The best position for an on-stage switchboard is prompt side. Each dimmer is controlled by a fader, a single, sliding, remote knob. The position of this knob is marked on the dimmer, from one to ten, which allows the lantern's intensity to be increased or diminished. By referring to the lighting cue cards, the operator can vary the intensity to create the desired atmosphere. As the dimmer is usually hired, the instructions must be studied carefully to make full use of the board's versatility: pre-sets, crossfades, black-out fader, and timing devices, etc., which can help the lighting team enormously.

Although stage lighting must at times appear very complex, its principles are quite simple: to light the players, to give the players dramatic impact, to blend and highlight the costumes and scenery. These principles are achieved by knowing how the lanterns function, how the dimmer controls the lights, how to set the right angle and amount of light, what colours to use, and, finally, what form or shape to give the beams of light.

Traditionally, light, brighter colours are associated with comedy and darker, more sombre colours with tragedy. Pantomime lighting should be bold and straightforward, the soft and subtle tones being reserved for dramas. Ghostly woods and palaces can be lit with blues and greens. In dance, the dancer's figure is the most important visual element and so the lighting should be aimed at the feet, knees, waist, and head. A silhouette back lighting with less front lighting is the ideal for this. Also, lighting low ground smoke on a bare stage heightens the atmosphere for dance.

For musicals, an overall cover of bright and colourful lighting is usually important. Revues can be lit in the same way, with many changes in the lighting plot to keep the tempo going. Traditionally, opera has no overall lighting, being only illuminated in parts: spots follow the principal singers. The other players are lit dimly in the background—heard but hardly seen.

Lighting theatre in the round presents problems. When positioning the lanterns care must be taken not to dazzle the audience, yet the players must be lit in whatever position they are on stage. A cover of 45° facing one another forms a circle neatly in four areas. A 60° coverage needs only three lights, thus saving the expense of hiring a further lantern.

Badly designed, wrongly applied lighting invariably disturbs the audience.

SPECIAL EFFECTS

Rain, snow, and lightning can be produced entirely by light projection, which can be obtained from theatrical stage-lighting companies. This equipment consists of a lantern, a motorized effect, and a projection system, and it can be erected on stands or hung from the grid on a spot bar (Figures 5.4 and 5.5). The disc-type projector has a glass disc housed between the lantern and the projection lens. This disc is driven by a motor via an adjustable friction wheel, which allows the speed of rotation to be varied. Various discs are available, including thunder clouds, fleecy clouds, storm clouds, rain, snow, running water, smoke, and flames. The box type of projector is similar but has no revolving discs. Instead it has a series of rippled glass plates that move slowly up and down on revolving cranks out of phase with each other. Behind the glass is the master-image transparency. Sea waves, water ripples, and undersea effects are available.

As mentioned previously, the gobo projector produces a fixed pattern from a cut-out metal plate. These can be made quite simply by stencilling (Figure 5.6).

Painted gauze or muslin is another lighting effect. A gauze painted in the normal way and lit from the front will appear quite solid but, when lit from the back, it will become transparent. This is ideal for pantomimes, revues, and musical and ballet effects, especially in transformation scenes. A further use of gauze is to hang it in front of the scenery to give it new texture (this is often done in professional opera). When using gauze in this way, all illumination should be from behind it, complemented with side lighting. Sometimes painted backgrounds create problems. The lights could reveal textures in the scenery that are detrimental to it or the shadows painted on it may cause the lighting team to reverse their ideas in order to light the set in the direction of the shadows. This problem can only be resolved by using flat light, which is not as exciting as angled lighting. A three-dimensional set, however, looks better when the light strikes it obliquely, giving it emphasis.

LIGHT INTENSITY AND COLOUR

Light levels are extremely important. A lantern with higher intensity than the others (known as the key light) gives an outdoor scene the feeling of light reflected from the sun or moon. When lighting an indoor scene, all lighting should appear to come from the windows and open doorways. Alternatively, a room may need to appear to be lit by domestic lights, fluorescent

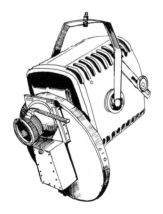

Figure 5.4 *Far right* Effects projector, 2,000 W, equipped with moving-effects attachments: thunder clouds, fleecy clouds, storm clouds, rain, snow, running water, smoke, flames, dissolving colours, chromosphere, and psychedelic

Figure 5.5 *Right* An adjustable floor lighting stand

Figure 5.6 Gobos

strips, etc. Gelatines (gels) must be taken into account when adjusting light levels: although they colour the set they reduce a lantern's intensity.

Gels are coloured, translucent, plastic sheets. Small book samples of gels are issued by stage-lighting companies, and the colours are known by names and numbers. They can be purchased in sheets or rolls and cut to size to suit individual requirements. Every lantern is equipped with a front groove or slot to house the gel in its frame (Figure 5.7).

Natural light is made up of many colours, so, if possible, white light should not be used alone. Sunlight effects are made by inserting amber gels, moonlight effects with blue ones, and ghostly atmospheres by green ones. Although all gels are fireproof they lose their effectiveness with use. Dark colours fade faster than lighter ones and therefore have to be replaced more often (this is because darker colours stop a high proportion of the light passing through them).

An elementary knowledge of colour is needed.

Figure 5.7 Cutting a gel (a chinagraph pencil is useful for numbering them)

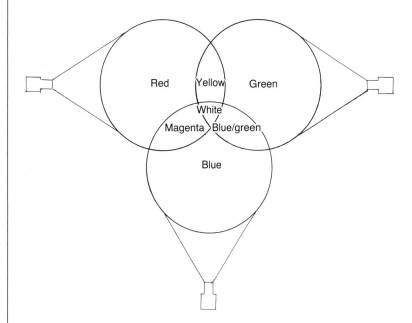

Figure 5.8 The lighting circle shows the mixture for white light: the three primaries, red, green, and blue. The secondaries are yellow, magenta, and blue-green. These also mix to produce white light. The three primaries are best used in cyclorama floods. Primaries may be too strong for small stages, and they also tend to change colour values. A red object lit by red turns naturally dark red; when lit by green it turns dark brown; but when lit by blue it turns into a dark purple. Green and blue lit by red turn black; when lit by green, a dullish green. Lit by blue, green turns black, and blue to a dark blue. Secondary magenta turns red when lit by red, blue when lit by green, and black when lit by blue. An alteration in lights can change the whole concept of scenery and costume

White light is made of the three primaries: red, green, and blue. The secondary colours are yellow, magenta, and blue-green, which, when mixed together, also produce white light (Figure 5.8). The primaries are often used in pantomimes, revues, and musicals to flood a cyclorama or other large background. Some colours tend to cancel each other out while others complement each other, especially darker tones. Lighter hues are used to improve the illumination of the player and the set. They create a 'natural' look and are therefore used more frequently than darker colours. Lighter colours warm the stage. Light levels also affect colour—warmer tones are produced at lower levels.

Gels can be combined and inserted into a single lantern to obtain different colours, but this will inevitably lower the light intensity. Different colours can also be put, separately, into one gel frame. Depending on the lens's focus, both colours will be projected or they will merge. Gels known as frosts (which are not coloured) are used to defuse a beam. These gels soften a hard-edged spot or spread the light over the whole stage.

Interesting shapes can be achieved using the profile, as its shutters move independently. Profiles are best for lighting specific areas. Shapes projected from gobos can also be very effective if coloured.

Figures 5.9 and 5.10 show how best to light faces on the stage.

MISCELLANEOUS LIGHTING EFFECTS

Other stage effects that come under the heading of electrics are any light-producing objects used in the play (household lighting, fires, televisions, lamps, candles, etc.). If these are wired to the switchboard, great care must be exercised as many appliances have only two-core cable while all theatre wiring has an earth.

For safety and also for good cueing, batteries with hidden switches can be used by the players themselves. Often, the switchboard technician cannot see the player and cues are often either delayed or anticipated. Batteries must be checked before each performance. When candles are lit in this way, the battery is housed in the candle's stem and a small bulb at the candle's top is covered with a twisted wisp of

Figure 5.9 Lighting a face from the four diagonals: (a) from the front lights up all the features but tends to flatten the face; (b) side light is dramatic but hides half the features, and the performer loses a great part of his or her expression; (c) top or back lighting does not produce a good effect; (d) lit from above and from in front, a much more interesting and dramatic effect is achieved; (e) if the player were playing the part of a genie, lighting from underneath or from the floor is very dramatic but is to be avoided for other roles as it gives an eerie atmosphere

Figure 5.10 Positioning of lighting for face illumination: (a) front (flat lighting); (b) side lighting; (c) from downstage right; (d) from upstage right; (e) top lighting (for a dramatic effect); (f) from top and front (good modelling illumination)

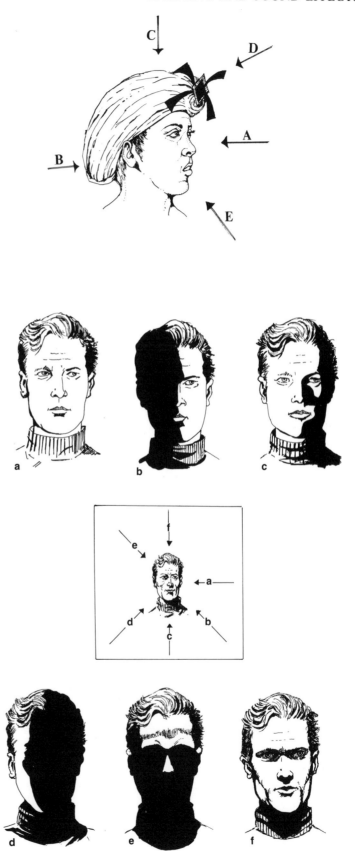

strong tissue paper to create the effect of a flame. The switch could be concealed in the holder. Care must be taken when the candle is 'blown out'. The areas around the candle must either be spotlighted from above or from front of house. Either way, this extra lighting must disappear immediately. Hand-held lanterns and torches can be treated in the same manner. All other switches, such as on-stage electric-light wall switches, should be easily visible to the switchboard operator.

When lighting an interior scene with such lighting, this must always be subservient to the lighting that lights the players' features.

SOUND EFFECTS

The effectiveness of sound is a vital part of a stage production. Sound effects can, nevertheless, make or mar the atmosphere of the play. It is important to position microphones and the amplification equipment carefully. Low-frequency sounds (non-directional) can penetrate objects or pass around them. Higher frequencies (directional)—because they vibrate much faster than most solid objects—are effectively stopped.

For theatre work, the reel-to-reel tape-recorder is the most useful. The tape-recorder operator must take care to keep all tapes away from any magnetic source or they could be completely spoiled. The recorder must be maintained regularly to keep it in good working order.

The microphones used in the theatre are of the moving-coil type because these are fairly strong and have good-quality tone value for human voices. The condenser type is a very delicate instrument but gives a good reproduction of most sounds. The ribbon type is not as popular as the other two and is sensitive only to sounds from the front and back.

The loudspeakers used must be capable of conveying sound throughout the whole auditorioum. Different speakers may have to be installed to produce the different wavelengths required.

Unless the sound equipment is loaned by a member of the theatre who knows its capabilities, the instructions that come with hired equipment must be closely adhered to.

Glossary

Acting area Space on the stage occupied by the performers.

Alb Priest's long white tunic.

Alginate Flexible dental moulding mixture that sets into a rubber-like compound when mixed with water.

Appliqué Applied or sewn-on motifs on costumes.

Apron (stage) Protruding part of the stage in front of the proscenium.

Apron Decorative feature for ladies' clothing, eighteenth century.

Back-cloth (backdrop) Scenic canvas battened top and bottom, the width of the stage.

Backing Usually booked flats placed behind doors and windows.

Backstage The area behind the proscenium arch.

Bacrooculus Roman, coarse, brown, woollen hooded cape.

Bar (lighting) Length of tubular iron hanging from the grid for securing lighting and scenic cloths.

Basque An extension of the corsage below the waist, nineteenth century.

Basquine After the sixteenth century, a fitted padded doublet; in the 1860s the name given to an outdoor lady's jacket.

Bavolet Frill or curtain at the back of the hat covering the neck, 1830s.

Beam light Parallel beam; without lenses.

Beards Spade—1570–1650 (shape of a pioneer's spade); marquisetto—1570 (close-cut); pickdevant—1588 (ends with point under the chin).

Bell hoop Under-petticoat distended with hoops, bell shaped; 1710–80.

Beret Cap with large halo crown heavily trimmed, 1820s–40s.

Bergère hat Lady's large straw hat tied on with ribbons; 1730s, 1800s, and 1860s.

Bliaut Close-fitting garment of the twelfth to early fourteenth century; worn by both sexes.

Blouse Loose garment of a different material from the skirt; second half of the nineteenth century.

Book flat Flats hinged together.

Box set Setting with only three walls, the fourth wall being the audience.

Braccae Type of breeches worn in Roman times.

Broad Bertha Wide collar reaching from neck to shoulder, seventeenth century and (as a revival) from 1839.

Bum roll Padded roll to distend the hips; second half of the sixteenth century and early seventeenth century.

Bustle Wire cage device to thrust the material of the skirt to the back; 1830s and 1880s.

Butt-end joint Method in scenery building; rail and stile placed end to end and nailed together.

Butterfly veil Wire frame supporting a gauze veil; second half of the fifteenth century.

Calash Large, folding, hooped hood covered in silk; named after the French carriage, Caleche, 1770– 90; revival in 1820–39.

Canions Upper part of men's hose reaching the knees and overlapped by stockings, 1570–1620.

Cannons Decorative frills to the tops of stockings, worn with the petticoat breeches fashion.

Cantilever box Contains the performer's makeup.

Centre line Imaginary line running down the centre of the stage to the proscenium arch.

Chaperon Short cape with hood; twelfth and thirteenth centuries.

Chemise Basic undergarment similar to a shirt; worn long and short by both men and women; thirteenth to the end of the nineteenth century.

Chemisette Muslin or cambric 'fill-in' to the bodice.

Chesterfield Overcoat named after the Earl of Chesterfield; 1830s–40s, then until the end of the century.

Chethomene Loose linen garment worn by the Hebrews in biblical times.

Chignon Hair at the back of the head arranged in loops or ringlets; second half of the eighteenth century.

Chiton Short tunic worn by the Greeks and Romans.

Clamp Device used to secure lamps to spot bars.

Cleat Metal or wooden hook pieces fitted to flats on right-hand outer stile to secure flats together by a cleat line.

Cod piece Front flap of the hose forming a pouch at the fork; fifteenth to sixteenth centuries.

Colour wheel Multicolour device automatically controlled; attached to lamps behind the lenses.

Colour frame To hold a coloured gel in front of a lamp.

Cope Priest's garment; a semi-circular cape fastened across the chest.

Corinthian Greek order.

Corner plate Small triangular piece of plywood nailed from rail to stile to strengthen the flat corners.

Cote Long-skirted tunic to below the knee; thirteenth century; worn by both males and females.

Cotehardie High-waisted garment with single skirt and hanging tippets; thirteenth century.

Crêpe hair False hair used by performers.

Cross piece Angled pieces of wood from top rail to stile for greater rigidity.

Cucullus Roman woollen cape.

Cut-out flat Profiled edge, often in plywood, projecting on the stage edge of the flat.

Cyclorama (skycloth) Usually a cloth stretched onto a curved frame; can be a straight cloth or a painted back wall.

Dagging Decoration by cutting borders of garments into various shapes; fourteenth to the end of the fifteenth century.

Dalmatica Garment shaped like a cross with a slit at the neck opening.

Décolletage Low neckline on ladies' dresses.

Dimmer Electrical apparatus to control lighting.

Doric Greek order.

Dormeuse hat Large, crowned, caul-type hat fitted loosely over the head; worn indoors; second half of the eighteenth century.

Doublet Short-style man's jacket; close fitting and tight waisted; fourteenth to seventeenth centuries.

Draperies Term used in the theatre for all curtains.

Farthingale Framework of hoops in a dome shape; sixteenth and seventeenth centuries; Spanish and French versions, the wheel farthingale, 1595.

Fitchets Pocket slits cut in front to allow access to purses beneath; fourteenth to mid-sixteenth centuries.

Flame drum Motorized drum stood in front of a lamp giving the effect of flickering frames.

Flat Standard construction of a wooden frame covered in canvas.

Flax Canvas used for scenic cloths.

Flies (grid) Area occupied by pulley blocks for flying scenic cloths or flats out of sight.

Flipper Very narrow vertical piece of scenery that supports the tormentor.

Floods Wide-angled lamps for illuminating large areas.

Floor plan Initial scale drawing of the stage area occupied by the set.

Follow spot Lantern that moves to follow the performers.

Fontange Female cap with tall erections of lace on wire, 1690–1710.

French brace Triangular wooden support bracket hinged to a flat.

Fresnel Spotlight fitted with a lens giving an even ray of light with soft edges.

Frock-coat Close-fitting male coat, buttoned to the waist with hanging tails at the back; end of the eighteenth to end of the nineteenth centuries.

Front-of-house lights Lights fitted in the auditorium.

Garrick (carrick) Long coat with multiple capes; eighteenth to nineteenth centuries.

Gauze Lightly woven material; transparent or opaque, according to the lighting positions.

Gelatine (gel) Colour filter used in lamps.

Gipon Quilted doublet worn under the cotehardie, fourteenth century.

Gobo Cut-out shape mounted in a frame and projected.

Grease paint Type of makeup used for the stage.

Ground plan Main plan of the stage area.

Groundrow Profiled piece of scenery, low lying as bushes, rocks, walls, or distant mountains.

Halberd Long-staffed axe weapon used in the fifteenth and sixteenth centuries.

Halving joint Method used in flat construction; cuts in rail and stile screwed together.

Hennin Lady's hat in a stiff, steeple-shaped cone; second half the fifteenth century.

Herygaud Voluminous garment, three-quarter length with wide sleeves, fourteenth century.

Hessian Loose-woven material for flats or backcloths.

Himation Long version of a Greek chiton.

Hose Trunk hose in the sixteenth century; after 1660 stockings.

Houppelande Long floor-length garment popular in the fifteenth century for both males and females.

House curtains (tabs) Curtains hanging immediately behind the proscenium.

House lights To light the auditorium.

Jerkin Loose jacket or doublet.

Kalasiris Egyptian rectangular piece of material with cut-out opening for the head; sides sewn up; made of a transparent linen gauze worn over the loin-cloth (shenti).

Lappets Hanging pieces from ladies' indoor headdress; the eighteenth to the nineteenth centuries.

Latex Rubber compound.

Leg-o'-mutton Sleeve of a lady's dress; full at the shoulders and tapering to the wrists; 1824 and a revival in 1896.

Liripipe Hooded cape with a long pendant tailpiece; 1350 to the end of the fifteenth century.

Love lock Long lock of hair from the nape of the neck brought over to hang down in front; 1590s to 1650s.

Mahl stick Short stick padded at one end to aid painting by steadying the hand.

Masking To hide backstage activities or lighting.

Merveilleuses (Les) French female trendsetters for the chemise dress, eighteenth century.

Mitre Bishop's headwear.

Mortise and tenon Method used in fixing joints in flat construction; the mortise is cut into the rail and the tenon into the stile.

Paenula Roman woollen cape.

Palla Roman lady's voluminous cloak held on each shoulder by a fibula or brooch.

Pannier Contraption of cane hoops in various styles, eighteenth century.

Papier mâché Method of using torn strips of paper pasted and applied either into a mould or over an object.

Parcan Lamp fitted with a par lamp.

Parti-colour Garment in contrasting colours.

Permanent set No movement of scenery throughout the performance.

Petasos Large sun hat worn by the ancient Greeks.

Piccadill Stiffened tabs for neck ruff; shoulder or waist for the doublet.

Platform *See* rostrum.

Plot The action of the play.

Profile flat Flat with the leading edge cut to a shape.

Prompt side Left-hand side of the stage.

Props Everything movable on stage except scenery, costume, and lighting.

Proscenium Arch piece dividing the spectators from the performers.

Postiche Ancient Egyptian Pharaoh's false beard.

Rail Top and bottom battens in a flat construction.

Rain box Large wooden box fitted with rows of nails in which dried peas are rolled.

Redingote Development of the wrap-over tunic, nineteenth century.

Risers Name given to the vertical part of a step.

Rostra Series of built wooden platforms.

Rostrum Single, built, wooden platform.

Ruff Circular collar of cambric or linen with a goffered frill; 1560s–1640s.

Sack gown Large shapeless gown, sixteenth century; revived in other forms in the seventeenth and eighteenth centuries.

Sash line Cleat line; thin rope attached to the back of the flat on the left-hand side of the outer stile to secure two flats together.

Scrim *See* gauze.

Set Completed arrangment of scenery and furniture.

Shoulder knot Bunch of ribbon loops worn on the right shoulder in seventeenth–century male fashions.

Sightlines Planned limits of audience's viewing.

Sill (iron) Narrow strips of iron that join the bases of doors, arches, fireplaces, etc.

Skycloth *See* cyclorama.

Snap-line Length of strong string covered in chalk or charcoal, held taut, then released to leave an impression on the canvas's surface.

Spatulas Wooden modelling tools.

Spencer Short-waisted coat without skirts, eighteenth century.

Spirit gum Used to fix false hair (e.g. moustaches, beards) to the performer's face.

Square up Transposing the squared-up drawing of the set to the back-cloth or flats.

Stage flashes (mag-puffs) Container filled with flash powder; automatically ignited.

Stage model Miniature setting in scale with the actual stage.

Stage platform Raised area of the stage.

Stage positions Theoretical division into areas; positions for stage directions.

Stage screw Large hand screw for fixing braces to the stage floor.

Stage weight Solid circular piece of metal to secure stage braces and French braces.

Standing set A set that remains in place throughout an entire production.

Stile Upright or vertical batten in flat construction.

Stola Long, straight tunic worn by Roman ladies.

Stomacher Ornamental chest piece; late fifteenth century, early sixteenth century.

Strike Dismantling the scenery and removing the props from the stage.

Sugar-loaf hat Hat with a tall conical crown with a flat or curling brim; sixteenth and seventeenth centuries.

Surcote Sleeveless tunic, twelfth century.

Tabard Circular material with centre slit for the head; late thirteenth century to the fourteenth century.

Tabs *See* house curtains.

Teaser Narrow border for masking the upper structures of the stage.

Theatre in the round Ground stage area surrounded by the audience with aisles as exits and entrances.

Thunder sheet Sheet of thin iron suspended by a rope and shaken by hand.

Tippet Early pendant streamers; then a short cape ending just below the waist, seventeenth century.

Toga Large piece of material wrapped around the body; worn by Romans of both sexes.

Toggle Wooden centre cross-piece in flat frame construction.

Top knot Large bunch of ribbon loops on the top of the head, eighteenth century.

Tormentor Narrow vertical piece of scenery to mask the wings.

Trunk hose Male breeches from waist to thigh; 1550s–1610.

Vinamold Hot-melting compound for making moulds.

Wind machine Wooden drum under a tightly stretched loop of canvas, turned by hand.

Wings Either side of the stage acting area.

Workshop Place of work, e.g. wardrobe department, props room.

Bibliography

Arnold, J., *Patterns of Fashion* (Vols. 1–3), Macmillan, London, 1972–85.

Barton, L., *Historic Costume for the Stage*, Boston, Mass., 1938; A. & C. Black, London, 1961.

Barton, L., *Period Patterns*, A. & C. Black, London, 1970.

Bentham, F., *Art of Stage Lighting*, New York, NY, 1968; London, 1980.

Bentley, E., *Theory of the Modern Stage*, Penguin Books, London, 1968; New York, NY, 1976.

Bradfield, N., *Historical Costumes of England 1066–1968*, Harrap, London, 1970.

Brook, P., *The Empty Space*, London & New York, NY, 1985.

Brooke, I., *Costume in Greek Classical Drama*, Theatre Arts, New York, NY, 1965.

Brooke, I., *Medieval Theatre Costume*, A. & C. Black, London, 1967.

Burris-Meyer, H. and Mallory, V., *Sound in the Theatre*, New York, NY, 1979.

Corson, R., *Stage Make-up*, Peter Owen Ltd., New York, NY, 1960.

Corson, R., *Fashions in Hair*, Peter Owen Ltd., London, 1985.

Cunnington, C. W. and P. E., and Beard, Charles, *Dictionary of English Costume 900–1900*, A. & C. Black, London, 1974.

Cunnington, P., *Costumes of Household Servants*, A. & C. Black, London, 1974.

Cunnington, P. and Lucas, C., *Occupational Costume*, A. & C. Black, London, 1967.

Cunnington, P. and Mansfield, A., *Handbook of English Costume in the 20th Century 1900–1960*, Faber & Faber, London, 1973.

Dorner, J., *Fashion in the Twenties and Thirties*, Ian Allan, Shepperton, 1973.

Dorner, J., *Fashion in the Forties and Fifties*, Ian Allan, Shepperton, 1973.

Earle, A. M., *Two Centuries of Costume in America 1620–1820* (2 vols.), Dover, New York, NY, 1970.

Fraser, N., *Lighting and Sound*, Phaidon Press, Oxford, 1988.

Goffin, P., *Stage Lighting for Amateurs*, F. Muller, London, 1938.

Govier, J., *Create your Own Stage Props*, A. & C. Black and Prentice-Hall, London & Englewood Cliffs, NJ, 1984.

Hill, M., and Bucknell, P. A., *Evolution of Fashion, Pattern and Cut from 1066 to 1930*, Reinhold, New York, NY, 1967.

Holt, M., *Stage Design and Properties*, Phaidon Press, Oxford, 1988.

Hope, T., *Costumes of the Greeks and Romans*, Dover, New York, NY, 1962.

Ingham, R. and Covey, L., *The Costumer's Handbook*, Prentice-Hall, Englewood Cliffs, NJ, 1980.

Jans, M., *Stage Make-Up Techniques*, Van Dobbenburgh, Amsterdam and Kidderminster, 1986.

Jones, E., *Stage Construction*, Batsford, London, 1969.

Kelly, F. and Schwabe, R., *Historic Costume 1490–1790*, Batsford, London, 1935.

Kohler, C., *History of Costume*, Constable, London, 1963.

Lambourne, N., *Staging the Play*, Studio Publications, London, 1956.

Laver, J., *Seventeenth and Eighteenth Century Costumes*, HMSO, London, 1958.

Melvill, H., *Theatrecraft*, Rockliff, London, 1954.

Melvill, H., *Historic Costume for the Amateur*, Rockliff, London, 1958.

Moore, J. E., *Design for Good Accoustics*, London, 1961; New York, NY, 1976.

Nelms, H., *Scene Design*, Sterling Publishing Co. Inc., 1970.

Oren Parker, W. and Smith, H. K., *Scene Design and Stage Lighting*, Holt, Rinehart & Winston, London & New York, NY, 1979.

Peacock, J., *Fashion Sketchbook 1920–1960*, Thames & Hudson, London, 1977.

Pilbrow, R., *Stage Lighting*, London & New York, NY, 1979.

Robinson, H. R., *The Armour of Imperial Rome*, Charles Scribner & Sons, New York, NY, 1975.

Russel, D., *Stage Costume Design*, Prentice-Hall, Englewood Cliffs, NJ, 1973.

Sichel, M., *Costume Reference Series*, Batsford, London, 1976–83.

Smith, R. C., *Book of Make-up, Masks and Wigs*, Rodale Press Inc., Emaus PA 18049.

Smith, R. C., *Book of Costume*, Rodale Press Inc., Emaus PA 18049.

Thomas, T., *Create Your Own Stage Sets*, A. & C. Black and Prentice-Hall, London and Englewood Cliffs, NJ, 1985.

Tilke, M., *Costume Patterns and Designs*, Zwemmer, London, 1956.

Tyrrell, A. V., *Changing Trends in Fashion*, Batsford, London, 1986.

Waugh, N., *The Cut of Men's Clothes*, Faber & Faber, London, 1964.

Waugh, N., *The Cut of Women's Clothes*, Faber & Faber, London, 1968.

Wilcox, R. Turner, *Dictionary of Costume*, Charles Scribner, New York, NY, 1969.

Yarwood, D., *English Costume from the 2nd Century BC to Present Day*, Batsford, London, 1975.

Suppliers

UK

Anello & Davide,
Drury Lane,
London W1
(theatre and ballet footwear).

Barnums,
67 Hammersmith Road,
London W14
(properties, make-up).

Bellman Carter (86) Ltd,
rear of 358 Grand Drive,
London SW20
(plaster, latex, and general
hardwear).

Bermans & Nathans Ltd,
18 Irving Street,
London WC2H 7AX,
and
40 Camden Street,
London NW1
(costume hire).

Brodie & Middleton Ltd,
68 Drury Lane,
London WC2B 5SP
(plaster, scenic paints, brushes,
etc.).

Fox, Charles H. Ltd,
22 Tavistock Street,
London WC2E 7PY
(theatrical make-up and wigs).

Hall & Dixon Ltd,
19 Garrick Street,
London WC2 9AX
(stage furnishings).

Leichner (London) Ltd,
436 Essex Road,
London N1 3PL
(make-up).

Morris Angel & Son Ltd,
119 Shaftesbury Avenue,
London WC2H 8AE
(theatrical costume hire and making
departments).

Newman Hire Co.,
16 The Vale,
London W3
(properties).

Old Times Furnishing Co,
135 Lower Richmond Road,
London SW15
(furniture, properties hire service).

Peter Evans Studios Ltd,
11 Frederick Street,
Luton,
Beds. LU2 7QW
(armour, masks, columns, pilasters,
etc., also vacuum forming, rubber
mouldings, glass fibre).

Rank Strand Electronic
PO Box 70,
Great West Road,
Brentford,
Middx,
TW8 9HR
(stage lighting).

Royal Shakespeare Co. (costume hire
department),
Royal Shakespeare Theatre,
Stratford-upon-Avon,
War. CV37 6BB
(costume hire).

Strand Glass Fibre,
Brentway Trading Estate,
Brentford,
Middx.
(moulding rubber and casting
materials).

Theatre Projects,
14 Langley Street,
London WC2
(lighting, effects).

**Theatre Sound & Lighting (Services)
Ltd,**
51 Shaftesbury Avenue,
London W1V 8BA
(lighting and sound).

Theatre Stop,
745 Sidcup Road,
London SE9
(costume and accessories hire).

Theatre Studios,
052/27 Clerkenwell Close,
London EC1
(properties).

Tiranti, Alec,
70 High Street,
Theale,
Reading,
Berks. and
17 Warren Street,
London W1
(moulding rubber, casting
materials, and sculpture tools).

USA

American Stage Lighting Co.,
1331 C. North Avenue,
New Rochelle,
NY 10804
(lighting).

Barris, Alfred,
156 W. 44th Street,
New York,
NY 10036
(wigs, beauty supplies).

Broadway Costumes Inc.,
15 W. Hubbard,
Chicago,
IL 60610
(costumiers rental).

Brookes-Van Horn,
117 W. 17th Street,
New York,
NY 10011
(costume rental).

Brudno Art Supply Co.,
601 N. State Chicago,
IL 60610
(brushes, artists' suppliers).

Chicago Costume Co. Inc.,
1120 W. Barry,
Chicago,
IL 60657
(costume rental).

Chicago Hair Goods Co.,
428 S. Wabash,
Chicago,
IL 60605
(hair, wigs, make-up).

Costume Collection, The,
601 W. 26th Street,
New York,
NY 10001
(costumes—only to
nonprofit-making organizations).

Costumes Unlimited,
814 N. Franklin,
Chicago,
IL 60610
(costume rental).

Craftsmen Speciality Supply,
6608 Forty Mile Point,
Roger City,
MI 19779
(metal, wood, plastics, castings).

Daniel's Co.,
2543 W. Sixth Street,
Los Angeles,
CA 90057
(artists' materials).

Eaves Costume Co. Inc.,
423 W. 55th Street,
New York,
NY 10019
(costume rental).

Electro Controls,
2975 S. 2nd West Street,
Salt Lake City,
UT 84115
(lighting, sound).

Electronics Diversified,
0625 SW. Florida Street,
Portland,
OR 97219
(lighting, sound).

Fishmans Fabrics,
1101 S. Des Plaines,
Chicago,
IL 60607
(fabrics, materials, etc.).

Garden Pharmacy,
1632 Broadway,
New York,
NY 10019
(make-up).

General Electric Co.,
Lamp Department,
Nela Park,
Cleveland,
OH 44112
(lighting).

Herman Leis & Son,
6729 W. North Oak Park,
IL 60302
(wigs, etc.).

ISLE Laboratories Inc.,
10009E Toldeo Road,
Blissfield,
MI 49228
(polyurethane foam and latex
casting materials).

Kalinsky, S. & Son Inc.,
156 Fifth Avenue,
New York,
NY 10010
(wigs).

Kelly, Bob, Cosmetics,
151 W. 46th Street,
New York,
NY 10036
(make-up, wigs).

Leichner Make-up,
599 11th Avenue,
New York,
NY 10036
(make-up).

Michael's Art,
Draughting and Crafts,
1518 N. Highland Avenue,
Hollywood,
CA 90028
(artists' materials).

Norcosto Inc.,
3203 N. Highway 100,
Minneapolis,
MN 55422
(costumes, props).

Nye, Ben, Inc.,
11571 Santa Monica Boulevard,
Los Angeles,
CA 90025
(make-up).

Pearl Paint,
308 Canal Street,
New York,
NY 10013
(artists' suppliers).

Peter Wolf Associates Inc.,
3800 Parry Avenue,
Dallas,
TX 75226
(costume, props, make-up).

Rosco,
36 Bush Avenue,
Port Chester,
NY 10573
(Rosco-Haussman scenic brushes).

Schoener, John,
2521 W. Berwyn,
Chicago,
IL 60625
(shoes).

Selan's,
32 N. State,
Chicago,
IL 60602
(wigs, etc.).

Showco,
9011 Governor's Row,
Dallas,
TX 75247
(lighting, sound).

Stage-Craft Industries,
1302 Northwest Kearney Street,
Portland,
OR
(costume, props).

Theatre Production Services,
59 4th Avenue,
New York,
NY 10003
(costume, props, make-up).

Tobins Lake Studios Inc.,
2650 Seven Mile Road,
South Lyon,
MI 48178
(vacuum-formed armour, costumes,
props, make-up).

Vogue Fabrics,
718–732 Main,
Evanstown,
IL 60202
(fabrics, materials, etc.).

Western Costume Co.,
5335 Melrose Avenue,
Hollywood,
CA 90038
(costume rental).

Index

Page numbers in *italic* refer to illustrations

Acting area 9, *11*, 14
Adhesives 11, 13, 31, 33, 89, 105
Apron (stage) 8, 11, 15, *15*

Backcloth 6, 8, 19, 23, 25, 26
Basque 58, 72, 74
Belts 37, 48, 50, 52, 54, 76
Blouses 73, 74, 75, 76
Bodices 53, 54, 55, 56, 58, 59, 61, 62, 64, 65, 66, 67, 71, 72, 73, 74
    jacket bodice 72
    underbodice 58, 61
Breeches 43, 46, 48, 56, 59, 61, 67, 68, 70, 75
    Rhinegraves *60*, 61
Brushes (scenery) 21, 23, *24*, 25, *25*, 27, 33
Bustle 58, 59, 61, 66, 72

Canvas 6, 15, 16, *17*, 18, 19, 21, 23
Cape *35*, 37, 40, 43, 45, 49, 50, 55, 59, 60, 67, 69
Capitals and columns 22, 23
Casting
    cold-cure rubber 120, 121
    metal 121
    sand 121
Chemise 48, 49, 50, 51, 53, 54, 56, 57, 59, 62, 66
Clay modelling 105, 115, 118, 120
Cleat 15, *16*, *17*, 18
Cloak 36, 38, 40, *40*, 43, 45, 46, 48, 50, 52, 55, 59, 61, 65, 68, 69, 72
Coats 60, 66
    box 69
    Brandenburg 61
    cassock 59
    Chesterfield 72, 73
    frock 67, 68, 70, *71*, 72
    Garrick 69
    Gladstone 72
    great 66, 67, 68
    Inverness 72
    morning 72
    overcoat 61
    Raglan 73, 76
    riding 72
    Ulster 73
    walking 72
Collars 47, 52, 54, 55, 58, 59, 67, 68, 72, 73, 75, 76
    Bertha 59
    falling 59, 66
    Medici 57
    Peter Pan 73
    roll 66, 70

stand-fall 67
standing 55, 57, 58, 59, 67
Costume types
    alb 47
    Anglo-Saxon *47*, *48*
    Assyrian 40
    bathing 74
    Beau Brummel *70*
    Belle Epoch 73
    Biblical 33, *37*, 38
    bliaut *46*, *46*, 48
    Byzantine 40
    chiton 37, 38, 39, *39*, *41*
    chlamys 38, *40*
    Classical 36
    ecclesiastical 47, *49*
    Egyptian 33, 34, *34*, *35*
    eighteenth-century *63*, 64
    Greek 36, 40
    Incroyables and *Merveilleuses* 64
    motoring 73
    nineteenth-century *68*
    Persian 40
    Pharaohs 34, *34*
    riding habit 67
    Roman 36, 40
    Russian *75*, 76
    tennis 75
    twentieth-century *74*
Cotehardie 50, 52, 53
Crinoline *71*, 72
Cuffs 50, 59, 64, 66, 68
Cyclorama 8, 19, 23, 28, 29, *29*, 130, 134

Dalmatica 39, 43, 47
Décolletage 53, 54, 57, 58, 61, 64, 65, 66, 71, 74
Doublets 50, 52, 53, 54, 55, 56, *56*, 57, 58, 59, 60
Drapes 8, 14, 15, 26
Dresses 58, 61, 62, 63, 71, 72
    day 67
    evening 74, 76
    hooped 65
    over 53, 74
    pelisse 69
    trained 67
Dyes 26, 33, 34

Farthingale 57, 58
Flats 15, 16, *16*, 18, 19, 21, 23, 25, 26
    book flat 15, *17*, 18, *18*
    flipper 15, *17*
Footwear 30, 70, 74, *84*, *85*
Furniture
    Anglo-Saxon 106, *106*
    Edwardian 110
    Egyptian 105, *105*, 109

eighteenth-century *108*
Elizabethan 106, 107, *107*
Georgian 107, 110
Greek *105*, 106, 109
Gothic 106, 107
Jacobean 106, *107*
Medieval 106, 109
nineteenth-century *109*, *110*
Norman 106, *106*
Regency 108
Restoration 107, 110
Roman *105*, 106
Romanesque 106, *106*, 109
Victorian 108, 110

Gauze 19, 35, 36, 132
Girdles 35, *35*, 38, 39, 45, 47, 48, 51, 54, 55, 59, 65, 66
Gowns 47, 51, 52, 53, 54, 57, 58, 59, 60, 62, 63, 64, 74
Groundrows 8, 29, *29*
Ground plan 9, *10*, 11

Hair and hairstyles 45, 94, 96, 98, 102, *102*, *103*, 115
    beards 90, 98, 99, 100, 113, 115
    Egyptian 98
    crêpe 89, *89*, 90, *90*, 94
    pieces 91, 97
    Roman 45
    wigs 47, 80, 90, 94, 96, 97, 98, 99, 100, 101, *101*
Hats, headwear and headdresses 77, 78, 79, *81*, 82, *83*
    Anglo-Saxon 77
    bavolet 80, 82
    bergere hat 79
    bonnet 77, 78, 80, 82
    bowler hat 78, 80, 82
    cap 77, 78, 79, 80, 82
        dormeuse 80
        mob 79
        pinner 79
        Phrygian 77
        under 79
    Cavalier hat 79
    chaperone *51*, 77, 78
    coif 77, 78, 79
    Egyptian 77, *77*
    eighteenth-century 79, *81*, 82
    fifteenth-century 79
    fontange 79
    Greek 77, 78
    helmet *41*, 77, 80, *86*, *112*, *125*
    homburg 82
    hood 36, 40, 43, 45, 46, 50, *51*, 52, 65, 78
    liripipe *51*, 77

Macaroni 80
medieval 77
mitre hat 49
nineteenth-century 80, *83*
Norman 77
petasos *40*, 77
Renaissance 77
Roman 77
seventeenth-century 79, *82*
sixteenth-century 78, 79, *81*
straw 75, 80, 82
sugarloaf 78, 79
top 80, 82
trilby 82
turban 78, 80
veil 45, 73, 77, *78*, 80
wide-awake 80, 82
wimple 77
Hinges 15, 18, *18*
Hoops 62, 63, 64, 67, 72
Hose 54
    trunk 56, *56*
    parti-coloured 50, *52*
houppelande 52, *53*, 54

Iron door sill *18*, 21

Jacket 67, 72, 73, 75
Jerkin 54, 55, *55*, 59
Jewellery 38, 40, 57, 64, 126, *126*
Joints 15, 16, *16*

Kalasiris 35, *36*
Kirtle 50
Knickerbockers 72, 74

Latex 105, 116, 118, *118*, 119, 121, 122
    adhesive 31
Lighting 6, 9, 28
    battens 130
    beam light 131, *131*
    designing 131, 132
    dimmer 131
    floodlight 129, *129*, 130, 131
    Fresnel 130, 131
    front-of-house lights 131
    gauze 132
    gelatine (gel) 133, 134
    gobo 130, 131, *133*
    lantern 129, 130, *130*, 131, 132, 133, 134, 136
    Parcan 131
    period 128, 129
    profile spot 130, *130*, 134
    projector lamp 29, *132*
    quartz-halogen bulbs 129
    safety 128
    spotlight 129, 131
    switchboard 128, 131, 136
    ultra-violet 131

Loin cloth (shenti) 34, 35

Make-up 6
    ageing 93, 94
    artificial blood 96
    black performers 93
    disfigurements 95, *95*
    false features 94
    gelatine 96
    liquid plastics 95
    men 91
    putty 93, 94, 95, *95*, 96
    rubber cap 96, 97
    spirit gum 94, 96
    straight 91
    tooth enamel 94
    wax 95
    women 92
Measurement chart 87
Model-making tools *11*, *12*
Modesty piece 64, 65
Monks 47, 49
Moulding 13, 28
    face *28*, *113*
    head *114*, *116*, *117*, *118*, *119*

Paint rollers 26, *27*
Painting methods 25, 27, 33
Panniers 63, 67, 73
Pantaloons 61, *62*, 67, 68, 70, 71
Papier mâché 86, 105, 110, 111, *112*, 118
Patterns 34, *35*, *36*, *37*, 38, *39*, *40*, 43, 45, *47*, *48*, *49*, 51, *53*, 56, 60, 62, *63*, *69*, *71*, *74*, *75*, 76
Peplos 36, 37, *38*
Petticoats 57, 58, 59, 60, 61, 62, 63, 64, 66, 71, 72, 73
Plasticine 120
Plaster of Paris 105, 112, 114, 116, 117, 120
Plays
    Biblical 38
    Elizabethan 107
    Restoration 107
    Shakespearian 8, 39, *22*, *23*, *32*, *55*
Polyester resin 105
Polystyrene 105, 121, 122
Polyurethane foam 121, 122
Proscenium arch 8, 11, 15

Rail 15, 16, 18
Robe 61, 64, 66
Rostrum *10*, *19*, *20*, *21*
Ruffs 55, 56, *57*, 58, *59*, 67, 69

Sash line 16

Shirt 40, 46, 49, 50, 59, 61, 71, 75, 76
    T-shirt 33
Skirt *35*, 36, 46, 50, 53, 54, 55, *57*, 58,

59, 60, 61, 63, 64, 66, 67, 71, 72, 73, *74*, *75*, 76
    gored 72
    hobble 73
    over 58, *59*, 66
    under 66, 71
    wrap-over 73
Skycloth 8, 130
Sleeves 35, 39, 43, 45, 46, 48, 50, 51, 52, 60, 61, 62, 64, 66, 68, 72, 76
    hanging 54, 55, *57*, 58, *59*
    leg-o'mutton 55, 67, 73
    Magyar 73
    slashed 54, *55*, 57
    trunk 55
    under 72
Snap line 25, 28
Soldiers
    Greek 39, *40*, *41*, *42*
    Roman 39, *44*, *45*
Sound effects 136
Special effects
    breakable props 122, 123
    cobwebs 122
    dry ice 14, 124
    explosions 124
    fire and smoke 123, 124
Square up 21, 23, 25, 26
Stage
    model *12*
    plan *12*
    positions 9, *15*
    properties 6
    sight lines 7, 9, *11*, 14
    standing set 8
Stile 15, 16, 18
Stockings 48, 50, 56, 71
Stomacher 58, *59*, 61, 63
Suit, American lounge 75
Surcote 50, 51, 53, 60, 61

Tabard 50
Teaser 15, *17*
Theatre-in-the-round 9, 11
Tippets 50, 59, 60, 69
Togas 38, 39, *43*, *45*
Tormentor 15, *17*
Trousers 39, 67, 72, 73, 75
Tunics 36, 39, 40, 43, 45, 46, 47, 48, 50, 54, 74

Vases *111*, *112*, 122
Vinamold 119, 120

Waistcoat 59–61, 67, 68, 70, 72, 75
Weapons *42*, 125, *126*, *127*
Wigs 30, 47, 58, *58*, 61, 66, 80
Wings (stage) 8